More critical praise for *Pension Fund Excellence:*

"This book sets the standard for Pension Fund Management for years to come. It is a must for pension fund trustees and officers both in the U.S. and Europe."

Jean M. G. Frijns
Chief Investment Officer
Algemeen Burgerlijk Pensioenfonds

"All pension fiduciaries, pension managers, participants, beneficiaries, regulators, labor leaders, or publicly held enterprise mangers, should read this book—it is a brilliant work on the role of patient pension capital and the responsibilities and liabilities of pension fiduciaries."

Dallas L. Salisbury
President
Employee Benefit Research Institute

"This book is full of marvelous insights and constructive thinking which anyone involved in pension fund investment will find invaluable."

Geof Pearson
Pensions Manager, J Sainsbury plc
Chairman, UK Pensions Investment Forum

PENSION FUND EXCELLENCE

WILEY FRONTIERS IN FINANCE

SERIES EDITOR: Edward I. Altman
New York University

PENSION FUND EXCELLENCE
Creating Value for Stakeholders

Keith P. Ambachtsheer
D. Don Ezra

John Wiley & Sons, Inc.
New York • Chichester • Weinheim • Brisbane • Singapore • Toronto

For my parents, Pieter and Wilhelmina; My wife, Virginia;
And my children, Julie, Jane, and Peter.

K.P.A.

I dedicate this book with gratitude to the foundations of my world:

Mercia and Esmond Ezra, for the love and care you put into raising me,
and the values I formed from your actions;

Margaret and John Dalgetty, for generously giving me the rare fortune of a second
loving family;

Jane and George Russell, for creating a professional environment in which I thrive,
doing what I like most.

D.D.E.

This book is printed on acid-free paper. ∞

This publication is designed to provide accurate and authoritative information in regard to the
subject matter covered. It is sold with the understanding that the publisher is not engaged in
rendering professional services. If professional advice or other expert assistance is required, the
services of a competent professional person should be sought.

Library of Congress Cataloging-in-Publication Data:
Ambachtsheer, Keith P.–
    Pension fund excellence : creating value for stakeholders /
by Keith P. Ambachtsheer, D. Don Ezra.
        p.   cm.
    Includes index.
    ISBN 0-471-24655-7 (cloth : alk. paper)
    1. Pension trusts—Management.   2. Pension trusts—Investments.
3. Pension trusts—Evaluation.   4. Pension trusts—Law and
legislation.   5. Trusts and trustees.   6. Fiducia.   I. Ezra, D.
Don.   II. Title.
HD7105.4.A58   1998
332.67′ 254—dc21   97-45105

Printed in the United States of America.

10 9 8 7 6 5 4 3

Preface

WHAT THIS BOOK IS ABOUT

There was a time when pension funds were an obscure subject, discussed only by obscure people. This is no longer the case. Seldom does a day go by when pension funds are not in the news for one reason or another. This is especially true in developed countries such as the United States, Japan, the United Kingdom, Canada, Switzerland, the Netherlands, and Australia, where the bulk of the globe's $12 trillion pension asset treasure trove resides. However, the rest of the world is paying attention, too. For example, the Chilean pension system is being widely touted as the quick route to building national pension wealth where none now exists.

However, being in the news is one thing, being understood is another. Thus far, the rising visibility of pension fund issues has not been matched by a broadened understanding of what pension funds do, how well they do it, and how they could improve their performance. This lack of understanding does not just reside on Main Street. It goes deeper. It exists among legislators and regulators. It exists in the media. It exists inside the financial services industry. Worst of all, many of the governors of pension funds themselves do not have a good grasp of what they are governing, and what it takes to do a better job.

What has caused this disturbing state of affairs? It exists because there has been no guiding paradigm that pulls all the strands of pension governance, finance, and investments together into a unifying, tangible, transparent whole. The goal of this book is to do just that. We assert that a pension fund is a special sort of financial business that needs to be managed in a businesslike fashion in the best interests of all its stakeholders; that is, those who have a financial stake in the fund's ultimate success.

OUR METHOD

Mindful of McLuhan's dictum "the medium is the message," we have worked hard to be businesslike in achieving the goal of this book too. We started by identifying whom we were writing for. The book's primary audience comprises those charged with the responsibility to create value for pension fund stakeholders. They are the "pension fund fiduciaries" we address in the book. Next, we agreed on the kind of book we wanted to write for them. It would be an intelligent, high-level, conceptual book using everyday, understandable language. It would be neither another "the great pension hi-jack" thriller, nor another "the ABCs of pensions" drone. If we could achieve this goal, a much wider audience would likely find the book valuable and interesting.

When we finished writing the first draft of the manuscript and sorted through the many insightful comments of its reviewers, we realized that the book fell naturally into five related, but distinct parts. The "business excellence" paradigm and the fact that there might be a global "excellence shortfall" approaching $60 billion per year is the focus of Part One. Next comes "What Every Pension Fund Fiduciary Should Know" (Part Two). The reason too many funds have poor business practices is that too many fiduciaries "don't know what they don't know" about pension economics, capital markets, and the market for investment management services. Part Two has separate chapters on each of these three areas.

Part Three, "Managing the Pension Fund Business," is the heart of the book. There are separate chapters on fund governance and organizational design, funding policy, asset allocation policy, policy implementation, results measurement and disclosure, and the special challenge of managing small pension funds. In Part Four, we transition from saying to doing. As experienced advisers to pension funds around the world, we have developed a good sense for best practices in pension fund management. We examine four actual cases to show how such practices are implemented. In Part Five, we look ahead into the twenty-first century and discuss three critical pension issues: the rise of defined contribution plans, the problems that plague national pension schemes, and the growing economic power of pension funds.

ABOUT THE AUTHORS AND HOW THIS BOOK WAS BORN

We both had the good fortune of starting our professional careers in the late 1960s, when the basic elements of what we might today call "pension fund capitalism" began to emerge. Capital markets and portfolio theory began to impact real-world investing and investment markets. Pension funds began to have separate lives outside the banking and insurance industries. Pension laws and regulations began to shape the unique legal environment in which pension funds operate. When we first met in Toronto in 1977, we discovered in each other early students and chroniclers of the pension fund capitalism phenomenon. We have been comparing notes ever since.

Ezra became the first formal chronicler with his book *Understanding Pension Finance and Investments* (Toronto: Pagurian Press, 1979), with Ambachtsheer serving as one of the manuscript reviewers. After working together as pension fund consultants at Pension Finance Associates for four years, it was Ambachtsheer's turn with *Pension Funds and the Bottom Line,* (Homewood, IL: Dow Jones-Irwin, 1986) while Ezra was one of the manuscript reviewers. Although both continued as prolific writers on pension governance, finance, and investment topics over the ensuing years, the topic of another book did not surface again until August 1996. We quickly decided the time had come, and that we would do this one together.

With our many other responsibilities and commitments, it took almost a year to produce the first manuscript. Then we asked for help. At the end of July 1997, we sent the manuscript out to 30 people and totally unreasonably asked for their comments within three weeks. Incredibly, 21 responded within the deadline. Then, as the two authors came together in the last week of August 1997 at the Ambachtsheer farm outside Toronto, a miracle happened. The collective wisdom of the 21 responses showed us the way to move from an interesting, but flawed manuscript, to the book we had set out to write 12 months earlier. Four grueling days of discussing, cutting, pasting, discarding, and rewriting later, the work was done.

We hope you like the result.

KEITH P. AMBACHTSHEER
D. DON EZRA

Acknowledgments

We are indebted to many people for their contributions to making this book a reality.

There were the formative, early contacts with mentors and former colleagues such as Peter Bernstein, Brendan Calder, Marty Leibowitz, Bob Mitchell, Bill Sharpe, Jack Treynor, and George Vilim.

And then there are the clients, past and present. Indirectly, they are the financiers of this book. Also, they provided the focal point for our work. We wrote this book for them. As importantly, they were not passive bystanders in the process. They questioned. They debated. They even gave us their best ideas, free of charge!

Current colleagues and industry peers have been another indispensable source of questions, debate, and fresh ideas. We thank you all.

Next, there are the wonderful people who made specific, tangible contributions to the writing of this book. Help with specific chapters was provided by Jane Ambachtsheer, Bob Bertram, John Ilkiw, Mohamed Khaki, Jim Pesando, Gloria Reeg, Mary Robinson, Hans Roos, and Masa Tsuno. We received helpful comments on an earlier manuscript as a whole from Craig Boice, Mike Clowes, Charlie Ellis, Jean Frijns, Pat Lipton, John MacMurray, Bob Monks, Peter Scurlock, Ross Steeves, Sara Teslik, and Ann Yerger. Some generous contributors even combined general manuscript comments with specific chapter suggestions. Thank you, Richard Ennis, Ken Gamble, Jack Gray, Sandy Halim, Claude Lamoureux, Burt Malkiel, Ryujiro Miki, Dallas Salisbury, Tom Scheibelhut, and David Slater!

Karen Chadwell undertook the daunting task of converting the many chapter drafts coming from two different word processors into a single, legible, clean manuscript. We still don't know how she did it.

The Wiley editorial team of Myles Thompson, Mina Samuels, and Sasha Kintzler were a delight to work with. Nancy Marcus Land and the team at Publications Development Company were equally competent. They understood what we wanted to do and provided all necessary support along the way.

Finally, we pay tribute to our families. It is difficult to imagine how we could have written this book without their unwavering interest and support.

K.P.A.
D.D.E.

Contents

PART TWO: WHAT EVERY PENSION FUND FIDUCIARY
SHOULD KNOW . . . OR HAVE A VIEW ON

PART THREE: MANAGING THE PENSION FUND BUSINESS

PART ONE
PENSION FUNDS AS FINANCIAL BUSINESSES
The New "Excellence" Paradigm

A pension fund is a special sort of financial business. To manage it as a business, the first job is to figure out in whose interest it should be managed, and who is to be accountable for results.

What distinguishes superior results from poor results, and how well are pension funds doing by such a standard? Research suggests there might be a global excellence shortfall approaching $60 billion per year.

How does the average pension fund get better at what it is supposed to do? Improved mission clarity and better organizational design are the keys to creating the excellent pension fund.

Chapter 1. The Coming Era of Pension Fund Capitalism

Chapter 2. How Good Is Pension Fund Management?

Chapter 3. Mapping the Road to Excellence

1

The Coming Era of Pension Fund Capitalism

> As we approach the twenty-first century, a remarkable convergence
> of political and economic institutions has taken place around the
> world. . . . This movement constitutes an end to history. . . .
>
> —*Francis Fukuyama*

CAN DEMOCRATIC CAPITALISM DELIVER THE GOODS?

As the twenty-first century approaches, the political and economic systems around the world are converging to a single, dominant structure: "democratic capitalism." Francis Fukuyama is only the most recent of a number of influential writers to make this point. Peter Drucker has written extensively on this theme. Joseph Schumpeter built the intellectual foundation for it in his seminal *Capitalism, Socialism and Democracy,* way back in 1943.[1] We argue in this book that the global convergence to democratic capitalism comes in the nick of time, for the developed world will soon face a new challenge—financing the physical and medical needs of the aging "boomer" generations in Europe, North America, and Asia.[2]

The political and economic institutions of democratic capitalism offer the best hope of meeting the financial challenges associated with the aging boomer generations around the globe. Especially critical will be the transformation of rising retirement savings flows into incremental wealth out of which rising retirement income claims can be met. The great economist Lord Keynes reminded us many years ago that increased saving by itself is only half of the answer to creating increased wealth. The other half is investment processes, which foster enterprises capable of efficiently producing goods and services which consumers want. In the end, only these enterprises, large and small, can ultimately pay the wages, taxes, and investment income necessary to keep democratic capitalism functioning in the twenty-first century.

THE CRITICAL ROLE OF PENSION FUNDS

We argue in this book that pension funds will be critical to successfully converting retirement savings into the wealth needed to support the much higher retirement income streams required over the 2010–2050 period.[3] But just as retirement savings by themselves are not enough to create wealth, neither is the mere existence of pension funds to take and invest those savings enough. Pension funds must invest in ways that produce positive bottom lines. They should aim to produce value for their stakeholders net of operating costs and adequate compensation for risk bearing.[4]

The bad news of this book is that many pension funds today do not produce enough of this kind of value. The good news is that the fiduciaries of pension funds can take a series of steps to predictably create value for their stakeholders.[5] This book explains these steps. Pension fund fiduciaries who follow these guidelines not only will strike a blow for the financial freedom of their own stakeholders. Collectively, they also will strike a blow for functioning democratic capitalism. The name of the game as we approach the twenty-first century is accelerated wealth creation. And that won't happen unless the majority of pension funds in the developed and developing economies focus on creating value for their stakeholders. We have entered the era of pension fund capitalism.[6]

COMING OUT OF THE CLOSET

Because they are relatively new financial institutions, pension funds haven't had the visibility and political clout of the banking and insurance sectors of the developed economies. This is now changing. The sheer magnitude of the assets, and therefore the importance and visibility of the pension fund sector in many of the developed countries, is now simply too large to keep them hidden in the closet. A recent study by Goldman, Sachs using InterSec Research Corporation data projects an aggregate pension assets value for the top 15 pension asset countries of US$12 trillion in the year 2000.[7] Table 1.1 displays the figures for the top eight countries. There is a further reason for the increasing visibility of pension funds. Over time, pension funds have become major repositories for the bonds issued by governments, and the bonds and shares issued by corporations. Thus without consciously seeking the role, pension fund trustees and managers have increasingly been thrust in the position of surrogate owners. Quite appropriately, this realization in turn has forced pension fund trustees and managers to focus on the financial performance of the government and corporate sectors. Good performance in the pension fund sector is impossible without good performances in the government and corporate sectors too.

Table 1.1 Pension Fund Capital Around the World in 2000 (Top Eight Pension Asset Countries)

	Pension Assets (US$ Billions)	Assets Per Capita (US$)	Largest Public/Industry Fund (US$ Billions, 1996)	Largest Corporate Fund (US$ Billions, 1996)
United States	8,078	$29,000	TIAA/CREF - $185	General Motors - $80
Japan	1,926	$14,000	Local Government - $82	Nippon Telephone - $16
United Kingdom	1,261	$21,000	Electricity Supply Group - $25	British Telecom - $34
Canada	607	$20,000	Ontario Teachers' - $37	Canadian National - $7
Switzerland	501	$69,000	Canton of Zurich - $10	CIBA-Geigy - $8
Netherlands	440	$27,000	ABP - $143	Philips - $16
Australia	242	$13,000	NSW State - $15	Telstra Super - $4
Germany	199	$2,000	N/A	Siemens - $14

Sources: InterSec Research Corporation, *Pensions & Investments.*

The asset values displayed in Table 1.1 do not tell the whole story. Pension funds are likely to increase their share of the financial sectors around the globe even further over the next decade for three reasons. First, the national pension schemes in the developed economies have historically been run on a "pay-go" basis, without serious funding. These pay-go policies are now being reexamined. The result could be either increased funding within national schemes, or conversion of the national scheme to compulsory private retirement savings arrangements.[8] Second, some of the large European economies such as Germany, France, and Italy have never required funding of their employment-based pension plans. These policies are also being reexamined.[9] Third, many of the developing economies are now jumping on the pension savings bandwagon as the surest way to build savings-to-investment transformation mechanisms within their national economies.[10]

CREATING VALUE FOR PENSION FUND STAKEHOLDERS

Pension funds around the world are the repositories of pension savings that have been accumulated to do two things. First, the setting aside of money now recognizes the cost of pensions tomorrow and creates the security that pensions anticipated will become pensions actually paid. Second, the return on pension savings is the major source of future pension payments.[11] The higher the return earned, the greater the source from which pensions can be paid. This in turn creates the option to either increase pension amounts, or reduce the cost of delivering the pension promised.

Who are the stakeholders in these pension arrangements? That depends very much on the formal pension arrangement between the plan sponsor and the pension plan participants (i.e., the "pension deal"). Most large-scale pension systems, whether national government or employer-sponsored, continue to be "defined benefit" based (DB). In this approach, plan participants typically earn pensions based on a common pension formula and years of employment. The ongoing funding of these projected benefits creates the pension fund. This fund holds the plan assets, which constitute the asset side of the pension plan balance sheet. These assets are invested according to a chosen investment policy, and implementation strategy.

The present value of the projected pension payments owed represents the outstanding debt on the liability side of the balance sheet. These defined benefit arrangements involve multiple stakeholders (typically pension plan members) and the plan sponsor, who in turn is ultimately backed by corporate debt and shareholders in corporate plans, or by public debt holders and taxpayers in public plans. Figure 1.1 lays out the issues surrounding these DB relationships schematically, using a balance sheet format.

Note that the first of the seven critical questions posed in Figure 1.1 is "What is the DB pension deal?" We show in this book that there is seldom a simple answer. Yet, the question must be answered. If the DB deal between the various stakeholders is not clearly articulated and understood (ideally by all plan stakeholders, but at least by the fiduciaries who are obliged to represent their financial interests), answering the other six questions becomes a logical impossibility. This doesn't mean, however, that a careful answer to "What is the DB pension deal?" will provide automatic easy answers to the other six questions. Indeed, it will take most of this book to examine how they in turn might best be answered.

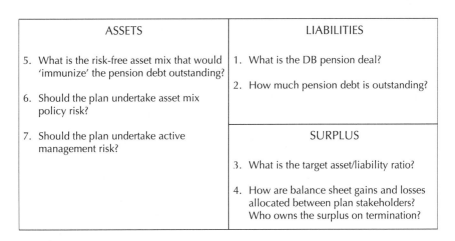

ASSETS	LIABILITIES
5. What is the risk-free asset mix that would 'immunize' the pension debt outstanding?	1. What is the DB pension deal?
	2. How much pension debt is outstanding?
6. Should the plan undertake asset mix policy risk?	
7. Should the plan undertake active management risk?	**SURPLUS**
	3. What is the target asset/liability ratio?
	4. How are balance sheet gains and losses allocated between plan stakeholders? Who owns the surplus on termination?

FIGURE 1.1   The DB Pension Plan Balance Sheet: Seven Critical Questions.

Many small-scale pension arrangements in North America, whether individual or employer-sponsored, are "defined contribution" based (DC), with the ultimate pension benefit based not on a formula, but on the amount of capital accumulated at retirement. In this arrangement, the stakeholder is solely the individual retirement savings plan participant, and there is no longer a guarantor of a defined pension based on a formula and years of service.[12]

Taking care to identify the stakeholders in pension arrangements is important, indeed critical. If pension funds are going to create value for stakeholders, the fiduciaries of these funds must be absolutely clear as to who the stakeholders actually are, and who bears which risks. Further, they must understand what kind of value these stakeholders want the fund to create. Only with these requirements in mind can the fund fiduciaries go on to devise and execute business plans designed to actually create that value.[13]

ON THE IMPORTANCE OF ACCOUNTABILITY

Much has been made in recent years of the importance of holding political and business leaders accountable for results if democratic capitalism is to deliver both freedom and wealth. An important message of this book is that pension fund trustees and managers must be held to the same high accountability standards if democratic capitalism is to "deliver the goods" in the twenty-first century. Accomplishing this goal requires careful foresight. Politicians are accountable to their electorate. Business leaders are accountable to their shareholders. We have already noted that pension fund fiduciaries must be accountable to the pension fund stakeholders. But how?

This book addresses the "how" question in considerable detail, and for good reason. Explicit mechanisms to facilitate accountability and transparency were not part of the original design of most national and employment-based retirement systems. So unless such mechanisms were inserted when their absence became apparent, they continue to be absent today. This renders pension funds especially vulnerable to "agency problems." Such problems arise when agents, in this case pension fund fiduciaries, are not explicitly motivated to create value for principals, in this case the pension fund stakeholders. Predictable consequences when agency problems are not solved include conformity in practices and mediocrity in results.[14]

Chapter 2 documents evidence that the pension fund industry may indeed suffer from these predicted consequences. Subsequent chapters show how to build accountability and transparency mechanisms into the management of pension funds, and how those mechanisms are platforms for launching business practices that create value for pension fund stakeholders. Getting it right is important. The very success of twenty-first-century democratic capitalism depends on it.

NOTES

1. See Francis Fukuyama's last two books *The End of History and the Last Man* (London: Hamish Hamilton, 1992) and *Trust: The Social Virtues and the Creation of Prosperity* (London: Hamish Hamilton, 1995). Peter Drucker has addressed the democratic capitalism theme in several of his books, including *Post-Capitalist Society* (New York: Harper Business, 1993). Joseph Schumpeter's seminal work *Capitalism, Socialism, and Democracy* (London: Unwin), was published in 1943.

2. The challenge of financing the needs of the aging boomer generations around the globe has been a major issue for specialists in the field for some time now, with the World Bank study titled *Averting the Old Age Crisis: Policies to Protect the Old and Promote Growth* (New York: Oxford University Press, 1994), one of the most definitive, and most frequently cited. Feature stories on TV and in the popular press, as well as massive advertising campaigns by financial services suppliers such as mutual funds, have helped make the issue a high-profile one in the developed world.

3. The leading edge of the European, North American, and Japanese boomer waves will be retiring in 2010 and will need retirement income for 15–20 years. The tail of the boomer wave will be retired by 2030. Thus the entire financing period stretches from about 2010–2050, with the 2020–2030 decade posing the greatest challenge.

4. This has become the best-practice standard for the corporate sector. Publicly traded corporate enterprises are expected to produce not just a profit for their shareholders, but a profit in excess of the cost of capital.

The American consulting firm Stern Stewart & Co. has dubbed this the positive "Economic Value Added" (EVA) standard. Chapters 2, 5, 11, 13, and 14 will elaborate on how this measurement discipline can be extended to the pension fund sector.

5. We will use the term "fiduciaries" throughout this book. By fiduciaries, we mean those persons legally empowered to make decisions regarding the pension fund organization, and/or the disposition of pension assets. Following the terminology introduced by John Ilkiw in his *The Portable Pension Fiduciary* (Toronto: Maclean Hunter Publishing, 1997), we discuss in subsequent chapters the roles of three types of fiduciaries: "governing fiduciaries," "managing fiduciaries," and "operating fiduciaries."

6. We are not the first to declare this the age of pension fund capitalism. It is somewhat ironic that over 20 years have already passed since the publication of *The Unseen Revolution—How Pension Fund Socialism Came to America,* by Peter Drucker (New York: Harper & Row, 1976). In it, he foreshadowed many of the ideas in this book. His use of the term "socialism" is interesting. We prefer "capitalism."

7. Exact, definitive pension asset values are hard to come by. Table 1.1 was constructed from projections published in *The Global Pension Time Bomb and Its Capital Market Impact,* by Mark Griffin, Goldman, Sachs Global Research, May 28, 1997. The projections were based on actual 1995 asset values estimated by InterSec. The 1995 actual values were projected forward to the year 2000 using demographic and stable pension plan funded ratio projections. These projections were made for 15 countries with aggregate 1995 assets of US$7.4 trillion. The projected combined asset value for the year 2000 is $12.0 trillion. The only change we have made to the InterSec-Goldman, Sachs projections is to increase the base 1995 U.S. pension asset value by $1 trillion to reflect IRA accounts, and the base 1995 Canadian pension asset value by $100 billion to reflect RRSP accounts. The InterSec data include all pension funds (except the noted IRAs and RRSPs) that can be allocated in the capital markets with some degree of freedom and are targeted for the provision of pensions. Largest fund asset values are as reported in the January 20 and September 15, 1997, issues of *Pensions & Investments.*

8. Canada, for example, has just decided to start funding its universal Canada Pension Plan. In contrast, Australia has decided to mandate pension funding through the employer sector, with employer and employee member contributions flowing into industry, corporate, or third-party-provided pension funds. The United States has not yet resolved how to fix its universal Social Security System, beyond stretching out the age of eligibility past

65 years. A number of proposals are being discussed, all the way from keeping the System intact but investing part of the Social Security Fund in equities, to winding down the System, and replacing it with a new system based on compulsory contributions going into individual retirement accounts. Japan has just launched a program of massive deregulation for all components of its retirement system. The goal is to raise the overall efficiency of converting retirement savings into future retirement income. The large continental European economies of Germany, France, and Italy have been the slowest off the mark in reforming their national pay-go pension schemes. However, the specter of looming insolvency will lead to action here too. Chapters 15 and 16 explore these developments in more detail.

9. There are efforts under way to standardize pension funding and investment rules across the European Community (EC) countries. For example, EC Internal Markets Commissioner Mario Monti is actively promoting the removal of restrictions to funding and investments across the EC. Meanwhile, pension plan sponsors in Germany, France, and Italy are moving ahead on their own. Sixteen major French companies through their research and lobby group "Pensions France" are promoting changes to French laws that would facilitate greater private pension growth in the country.

10. The Chilean national pensions scheme, started in 1981, is often cited as a major contributor to the rapid economic development of that country during the 1980s and 1990s. It is based on compulsory contributions by all working Chileans to the pension fund administrator of their choice. Not only has the scheme been imitated by other Latin American countries such as Peru, Argentina, Colombia, and Uruguay, but it is also becoming increasingly popular in the developing nations in the Near East, the Far East, and the former Soviet bloc. It is studied further in Chapter 15.

11. In the typical pension plan with typical investment experience, about 80 percent of its ultimate financial resources come from investment income versus only 20 percent from the original contributions.

12. Not all defined-contribution-based (DC) pension arrangements are small. For example the New York-based $185 billion Teachers' Insurance Annuity Association-College Retirement Equities Fund (TIAA-CREF) has a DC orientation. Also, the new Australian national compulsory contributions pension regime is creating large, DC-based pension plans there. See Chapter 15 for an in-depth discussion of DC pension systems.

13. Again, this statement foreshadows a more detailed discussion in subsequent chapters about the respective roles of governing, managing, and operating fiduciaries.

14. The Summer 1995 issue of the *Journal of Applied Corporate Finance* (Vol. 8, No. 2), provides an excellent review of the challenges of managing complex organizations where neither the managers nor the workers "own" the business. The challenge comes down to (1) correctly aligning decision authority with decision-making knowledge and skills, and (2) designing reward systems that align the economic interests of the managers and workers with those of the firm and its owners. The pension fund version of what can happen with the misalignment of decision-making authority and capability, and of the misalignment of the economic interests of principals and agents is described in somewhat overdramatized fashion in *Fortune and Folly: The Wealth and Power of Institutional Investing* by William O'Barr and John Conley (Homewood, IL: Business One Irwin, 1992). Its key findings are summarized in Chapter 2.

2

How Good Is Pension Fund Management?

After reading our book, you'll feel a little bit like the airline passenger who peeks into the cockpit at 30,000 feet and discovers there is no one there.

—*William O'Barr and John Conley*

AN ANTHROPOLOGICAL VIEW OF PENSION FUND MANAGEMENT

Anthropologists William O'Barr and John Conley caused quite a stir in the American pension fund management community with their 1992 book *Fortune and Folly: The Wealth and Power of Institutional Investing.*[1] The book was based on their observation of the managements of nine large U.S. pension funds over a period of two years, and as suggested by the lines cited at the beginning of this chapter, they arrived at some rather unflattering conclusions:

- While decision making at each of the nine funds had all the trappings of rigorous analysis, it in fact seemed to be more grounded in organizational culture and history, in how responsibility and blame might be deflected, and in how personal relationships might be affected.

- The organizational structure seemed in each case to be more a response to culture and history, rather than the result of a careful study of the mission-driven alternatives.

- The most pervasive cultural theme encountered was the need to manage responsibility and blame.

- An extraordinary amount of attention was paid to maintaining and nurturing good personal relationships with outside suppliers.

- There were powerful disincentives to both corporate and public sector fund managers to become actively engaged in corporate governance issues.

- Investing in foreign markets was reduced to a simplistic formula approach, without acknowledging the need to accommodate foreign cultures and business practices.

The American pension fund management community reacted to these conclusions with a mixture of disdain, denial, and disbelief. "O'Barr and Conley are just trying to sell books," said some. "What conclusions can one reach from a sample of only nine pension funds?" said others. "Anthropologists don't know enough about the intricacies of pension fund management to make any judgments about its quality," said still others. Nevertheless, O'Barr and Conley had struck a nerve. The practice of shooting messengers who bring bad tidings goes back a long way.

PENSION FUND MANAGERS BECOME
MESSENGERS THEMSELVES

That O'Barr and Conley were on to something was confirmed on December 7, 1994, in New York. Fifty of North America's most experienced and senior pension fund managers had gathered to attend an *Excellence in Pension Fund Management* symposium.[2] In the very first session of the day, the symposium organizers distributed a questionnaire to the attendees before they had even finished their first cup of coffee. "What is the cost of 'excellence shortfall' in your organization?" they were asked. In other words, "If your organization could somehow get rid of all the known blockages to excellence, how much do you think your fund's performance would improve?"

There was a wide range of responses. The middle value of the range is probably most telling: 66 basis points or 0.66 percent per annum. This is a material number. A realistic prospective long-term rate of return on the typical American pension fund today is probably a single-digit number.[3] Thus a 0.66 percent return increment now represents a highly material increase in fund revenues, and an even more material increase in the fund's after-expenses bottom line, and its ability to support higher pensions.[4] So maybe the response of the pension fund community to the message of O'Barr and Conley's book was not so much a matter of whether the kettle was black, but who got to call it black and why. O'Barr and Conley had darkly suggested empire building as the underlying motive, whereas pension fund executives see poor organizational design and poor decision processes as the problem.

MEASURING PENSION FUND VALUE PRODUCTION DIRECTLY

The accuracy of the subjective 66 basis points excellence shortfall estimate of 1994 received direct, quantitative confirmation in 1996. It came as the result of a study on the four-year, value-added production performance of 98 North American pension funds aggregating to about $750 billion in asset value.[5] As stated in this book, the study recognized that total pension fund performance comes from two fundamental sources: (1) the chosen asset mix policy for the fund, and (2) the way in which that policy is implemented.

The choice of asset mix policy involves multiple considerations, including the nature of the pension liabilities, risk tolerance, the funded status of the pension plan, long-term capital markets prospects, and current perceptions of the standard pension fund asset mix.[6] These factors make it difficult to assess after the fact whether a chosen asset mix policy was "good" or "bad." However, assessing the quality of the policy's implementation suffers from fewer ambiguities. Assessing the quality of implementation is a matter of assessing cost-effectiveness: What did the fund spend in terms of operating costs and incremental risk, and what payoff did it get for those expenditures?

Table 2.1 summarizes the calculations needed to answer the "what payoff did it get?" question, using the average experience of the 98 pension funds over the four-year (1992–1995) evaluation period. First, the funds' gross annualized returns were established. The average was 10.7 percent. From the gross returns, the estimated policy returns that would have been earned had the funds' asset mix policies been implemented passively were subtracted. They averaged 10.7 percent, leading to an average fund gross value added of 0.0 percent. Subtracting the funds' average annual incremental active management cost of 0.2 percent from gross value added leads to an average net value added of −0.2 percent. Finally, subtracting the average risk penalty of 0.3 percent from the net value added leads to an average risk-adjusted net value added (RANVA) of −0.5 percent.[7]

The average fund RANVA represents the amount of fund return left over after accounting for a fund's asset mix policy, incremental operating costs, and incremental risk assumption costs. The RANVA measure and the methods of calculating it are discussed further in Chapters 5, 11, and 13. Here we simply observe that Table 2.1 indicates that the average RANVA for the 98 pension funds over the four-year measurement period was −0.5 percent, or a negative 50 basis points per annum. Thus money was left on the table in the sense that the average fund would have been

Table 2.1 1992–1995 Average Risk-Adjusted Net Value Added for 98 North American Pension Funds

Gross Fund Return	10.7%
less Fund Policy Return	10.7%
equals Gross Value Added	0.0%
less Incremental Active Management Costs	0.2%
equals Net Value Added	−0.2%
less Active Management Risk Penalty	0.3%
equals Risk-Adjusted Net Value Added (RANVA)	−0.5%

Source: The Ambachtsheer Letter, No. 130, November 1996.

better off implementing its asset mix policy passively, and thus undertaking very little in the way of operating cost and active management risk in the process.[8]

SO WHAT'S THE PROBLEM?

Thus quite apart from the observations of anthropologists O'Barr and Conley, we have two independent indications that the typical North American pension fund may be experiencing a serious excellence shortfall in the neighborhood of, say, 0.5 percent per year. One was an educated guess by senior pension fund managers. The other was a quantitative confirmation through studying the actual operating performance of a sizable sample of North American pension funds. We know of no reason why the typical pension fund in the other developed economies should be systematically doing any better. Applying a performance drag of 50 basis points per year to a global pension asset base of $12 trillion suggests a global return shortfall on pension assets of as much as $60 billion per year. This is a serious problem in a world struggling to accumulate sufficient wealth to pay adequate pensions to retired boomers.[9]

So what is going on here? This was exactly the next question on the *Excellence in Pension Fund Management* symposium questionnaire. Specifically, the 50 senior pension fund executives were asked to list the major blockages to excellence that they felt their organizations faced. Again, there was a wide range of responses. However, Table 2.2 indicates that when these responses were organized into broad categories, the message was unmistakable. The number one blockage to achieving excellence in pension fund management is organizational dysfunction. This dysfunction manifests itself in a number of ways: lack of mission focus, poor decision processes, and inadequate skills and resources. These shortcomings in turn can lead to inappropriate financial policy decisions for the pension plan, and inappropriate organizational design decisions for the pension fund business.

The most interesting aspect of the responses categorized in Table 2.2 is that the pension executives agreed overwhelmingly that their problems were internal, not external. Notice, for example, that external factors

Table 2.2 Barriers to Excellence in Pension Fund Management: The Views of 50 Senior Pension Executives

Rank	Barrier	Cited (%)
1	Poor process (including structure, communication, and inertia)	98
2	Inadequate resources	48
3	Lack of focus or of clear mission	43
4	Conservatism	35
4	Insufficient skills	35
6	Inadequate technology	13
7	Conflicting beliefs	8
7	Difficult markets	8
9	Lack of innovation	5
9	Suppliers	5

Source: Excellence Shortfall in Pension Fund Management: Anatomy of a Problem, by K. Ambachtsheer, C. Boice, D. Ezra, and J. McLaughlin, unpublished Research Paper, October 1995.

such as "difficult markets" and "suppliers" were seldom cited as major barriers to excellence. Paraphrasing Pogo's famous observation, pension fund managers have seen the enemy; it is themselves and their governing fiduciaries.

MEASURING THE IMPACT OF ORGANIZATION DESIGN QUALITY DIRECTLY

The subjective views of the 50 pension fund executives regarding the relationship between organization excellence and organization design were confirmed statistically in 1997.[10] The pension fund CEOs for whose funds the organization performance metric RANVA was available, were sent an organization design quality questionnaire containing 45 statements which they were asked to score on a scale from 1 to 6. The 45 statements were designed so that for each statement score, a low assigned score indicated the CEO was unhappy with that aspect of organization design, and a high score indicated high satisfaction with that aspect. The 45 assigned scores were averaged to create an overall CEO organization design quality score.

The survey participation rate was high, with 80 out of 127 CEOs returning completed questionnaires. Remarkably, there turned out to be a statistically significant relationship between organization performance as measured by each fund's RANVA, and organization design quality as measured by each fund's overall CEO score. Even more remarkable are the findings displayed in Table 2.3. The Table lists the 11

Table 2.3   The 11 Drivers of Organization Performance

Statement Number	Statement
Governance	
2	My governing fiduciaries have good mechanisms to understand and communicate with plan stakeholders.
7	My governing fiduciaries do a good job of balancing overcontrol and undercontrol.
9	Our fund has an effective process for selecting, developing and terminating its governing fiduciaries.
13	My governing fiduciaries and related committees use their time efficiently (focused and do not waste time).
14	There is a high level of trust between my governing fiduciaries and the pension investment team.
15	There is a clear allocation of responsibilities and accountabilities for fund decisions between the governing fiduciaries and the pension investment team.
Planning and Management	
19	I can describe our vision of where we should be in the future.
22	I can describe our fund's strategic positioning (how we provide better value to stakeholders than alternatives).
24	I can describe our resource plan (obtaining and optimally utilizing the required human, financial and information technology resources).
28	Developing our asset mix required considerable effort on the part of myself and the governing fiduciaries and it reflects our best thinking.
Operations	
37	My organization uses its time efficiently (well focused and does not waste time).

Source: Organization Performance vs. Organization Design study, Toronto, December 1997. Conducted jointly by Capelle Associates Inc., Cost Effectiveness Measurement Inc., and KPA Advisory Services Ltd.

individual organization design quality statements where the CEO scores assigned to those statements were positively associated with the fund RANVAs at a high level of statistical significance.[11] Note that the 11 listed "drivers of organization performance" categorize themselves nicely into the top three barriers cited in Table 2.2. The cited "poor decision processes" there are echoed in Statements 7, 13, 14, 15, 28, and 37 in Table 2.3. Statements 9 and 24 relate directly to "inadequate resources," and Statements 2, 19, and 22 to "lack of focus or of clear mission."

What can be done to remove these internal blockages to excellence? Drawing a map of the road to excellence would seem like a good place to start. This is the task of Chapter 3.

NOTES

1. See Chapter 1, note 14.

2. The *Excellence in Pension Fund Management* symposium was organized jointly by The Boice, Dunham Group, Cost Effectiveness Measurement Inc., and Frank Russell Company for their clients. All three organizations provide advisory, consulting, and/or measurement services to pension fund managements.

3. This single-digit nominal (not real) return projection is based on the realities of prevailing 6 percent American long bond yields and 2 percent dividend yields on common stocks. Even if dividends grew by an exceptional 8 percent to produce a 10 percent long-term return on stocks, the expected return on a typical 60–40 stock-bond asset mix today would still be under 9 percent.

4. For a typical pension fund, the rule of thumb is that an additional 1 percent of return on assets can support a 15 percent increase in benefits, or a 15 percent reduction in contributions to support the current pension benefit. Applying this rule of thumb to an additional 0.66 percent of return, a 10 percent increase in benefits or reduction of contributions is implied. The point is that an excellence shortfall of 0.66 percent is material, and demands corrective action. As a standard of comparison, quality management experts use 20 percent as the typical improvement potential in moving from an average to an excellent organization.

5. These findings were documented in a series of *Ambachtsheer Letters* during the fall of 1996. The research involved 46 U.S. pension funds aggregating to

$600 billion in assets, and 52 Canadian funds aggregating to $150 billion. Cost Effectiveness Measurement Inc. provided the data. The *Ambacht-sheer Letter* is available by subscription from KPA Advisory Services, Toronto, ON, Canada.

6. See Chapters 4 and 9 for a detailed discussion of the considerations that should go into deciding a fund's asset mix policy.

7. The active management risk penalties for the 98 funds were calculated by charging a required hurdle rate on a fund's value at risk (VAR) due to active management. This VAR was estimated by calculating the standard deviation of each fund's annual "value-addeds" around their four-year means, and multiplying the standard deviation times two. See Chapter 11 for a more detailed discussion of the considerations that should go into how pension fund performance should be measured. There we show that the active management risk penalty could be calculated to come out as low as 0.0 or as high as 0.6 percent, depending on the assumptions used. Here we use the midpoint of the 0.0 percent to 0.6 percent range: 0.3 percent.

8. Implementing a fund's asset mix policy passively through publicly traded securities costs only a few basis points. A "basis point" is one-hundredth of one percent.

9. On one hand, it could be argued that our 50 basis points performance drag estimate might understate the global magnitude of the problem. The estimate is based on (1) the fund excellence shortfall guesses and (2) the fund RANVA achievements of arguably "the best and the brightest" in the North American pension fund universe. It is not unreasonable to surmise that the rest of the global pension fund universe has an even larger performance drag. On the other hand, the 50 basis points excellence shortfall may be an overstatement. We note in Chapter 12 that larger funds generally perform better than smaller funds. On a dollar-weighted basis, the excellence shortfall may be less.

10. The cited 1997 study was conducted jointly by Capelle Associates, an organization design consulting firm, Cost Effectiveness Measurement, a pension fund performance benchmarking firm, and KPA Advisory Services, a pension fund advisory firm. All three firms are based in Toronto, ON, Canada. The study was sponsored by 8 major pension funds, Algemeen Burgerlijk Pensioenfonds (ABP), AT&T Investment Management Corporation, California Public Employees' Retirement System (CalPERS), Florida State Board of Administration, IBM Corporation Retirement Fund, Ontario Municipal Employees' Retirement System (OMERS), Ontario Teachers' Pension Plan Board, and State of Wisconsin Investment Board. Table 2.3 was extracted from "Organization Performance vs. Organization

Design", a proprietary study prepared for the 8 project sponsors by the 3 firms which managed the project. The major findings of the study were published for a wider audience in an *Ambachtsheer Letter* dated December 19, 1997 and titled "Good Governance Matters Most."

11. The cut-off for the t-statistics was set at 2. This implies that the probability that each of the uncovered statistical relationships between fund RANVAs and the statement CEO scores being due to chance is less than 1 in 20.

3
Mapping the Road to Excellence

Two roads diverged in a wood, and I—I took the one less traveled by, and that has made all the difference.

—*Robert Frost*

PENSION FUNDS AS FINANCIAL BUSINESSES

The idea that pension funds are financial businesses that must create value for their stakeholders is not new. The authors of this book made the "run it like a business" paradigm a central tenet of their consulting practice as early as 1981.[1] Yet, the facts set out in Chapter 2 suggest that a considerable gap between the idea and the reality remains. At the same time, the much larger economic impact pension funds now have on their stakeholders and on the economy at large has increased the urgency of narrowing the gap. So what can be done?

Recent work in the field of organizational economics offers a fresh and promising perspective on the problem. This work explains, for example, why many organizations that genuinely want to improve their performance often fail to do so. The common culprit is poor organizational design, and the common solution is to fix it. Good organizational design starts by recognizing three principles: (1) "Decision rights" within the organization must be clearly assigned; (2) information systems must evaluate the "value production" of the overall organization, and its units; and (3) reward systems must provide incentives for all decision makers within the organization to create value.[2]

Obvious though these three principles might sound, too few pension fund organizations adhere to them. Decision rights assignment is often fuzzy. Information systems often measure the wrong things. Reward systems are often not tied to value creation. And the message from organization economics is that it is not enough to get one, or even two of the key principles of good design embedded into how the organization functions. All three must operate in concert.

THE MAP

Figure 3.1 lays out a map to organization excellence in managing pension funds. The heart of it is the organization design box with its three key principles related to decision rights, information systems, and incentive compensation. But there is more to it than that. The map makes it evident that good organization design is only a means to an end. The end is to create value for pension fund stakeholders. This requires incentives and actions driven by good organization design. Good organization design is driven by a clear organization mission, and the policies and strategies required to achieve it.

In turn, the organization mission, policy, and strategy decisions do not come out of thin air. They are made in the context of understanding stakeholder needs, the degrees of financial markets efficiency, the key principles of pension and investment economics, and of information technology, and the legislative and regulatory rules within which the fund operates. The map laid out in Figure 3.1 denotes all this as "key beliefs, principles, and constraints." The fund cannot operate coherently without clarity within the organization about how these considerations impact the excellent pension fund organization and its approach to managing the pension fund. They are pursued further in Chapters 4, 5, and 6.

The map also helps make a critical distinction between the governance, management, and operations functions in a pension fund. The focus for the

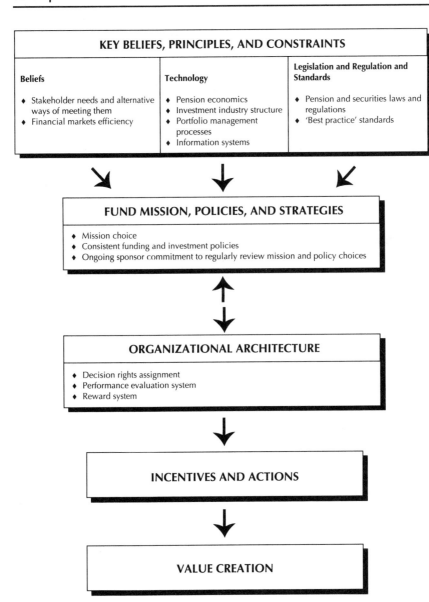

FIGURE 3.1 The Pension Fund Organizational Excellence Map. *Source:* Adapted from "The Economics of Organizational Architecture," by James Brickley, Clifford Smith, and Jerold Zimmerman (*Journal of Applied Corporate Finance,* Summer 1995).

governance function is mission choice, funding and investment policy decisions, organizational design decisions, the monitoring of organizational effectiveness, and communication of results to stakeholders. This is the domain of the pension fund governing fiduciaries. Management acts as advisers to the governing fiduciaries, devises strategies for achieving the fund mission and implementing the chosen policies in a cost-effective manner, and organizes and monitors fund operations. This is the domain of the management fiduciaries. Finally, fund operations in the form of portfolio management, risk monitoring, and information system management and reporting are delegated to operating fiduciaries either inside or outside the pension fund organization.

The map underscores that the board of governing fiduciaries is the fountainhead of any pension fund business. It is difficult to see how any pension fund can create value for stakeholders without an effective board.

THE BOARD OF GOVERNING FIDUCIARIES

If pension funds were publicly listed companies, they would be governed by boards of directors. As legal entities that operate under country-specific legal and regulatory umbrellas geared to oversee pension investing, pension funds are typically governed by a board of trustees, a pension committee, or its equivalent.[3] The members of this body, called the "governing fiduciaries" in this book, have the ultimate responsibility to define what "value creation" is in the context of a specific pension fund. This in turn requires the articulation of a mission for the pension fund, and a set of financial and organizational policies that will support the mission's achievement.

Doing these things well involves conquering difficult challenges that start with gaining a thorough understanding of the pension deal to be governed. This includes knowing who the pension plan stakeholders are, and how gains and losses on the pension plan balance sheet are to be allocated among these stakeholders. It means being knowledgeable enough to ask the right questions about the "key beliefs, principles, and constraints" listed in Figure 3.1. It requires making choices among competing policy options related to funding and investment policy. It calls for making organizational design decisions. Finally, it entails choosing a leader to manage the pension fund as a financial business.

Chapter 7 is devoted to the selection, organization, and functioning of effective boards of governing fiduciaries.

MANAGERIAL AND OPERATIONAL COMPETENCE MATTERS

A dedicated, competent board of governing fiduciaries is a necessary condition for excellence in pension fund management. But it is not enough. Figure 3.1 illustrates that even if the fund mission, its funding and investment policies, and its organizational design are right, the production of stakeholder value is not assured. Ultimately, it is the fund's managing and operating fiduciaries who will produce the hoped-for stakeholder value, or who won't. The selection of the fund chief executive officer is the critical first step in turning fund mission, policies, and organizational design decisions into stakeholder value.

A lot rides on this selection process. Competence is one obvious selection criterion. But again, competence by itself is not enough. There must also be trust. The 50 senior pension fund executives surveyed in the *Excellence in Pension Fund Management* symposium, discussed in Chapter 2, believed the barriers to excellence were to be found mainly inside the pension fund organization. The issue of trust looms large in and around their top three cited barriers to excellence: poor process, inadequate resources, and lack of clear mission. Only boards and chief executives who respect each other, and can work well together, have any chance of removing such barriers to excellence. Chapters 10, 13, and 14 look at pension fund management and operations in further detail.

CREATING VALUE IN PENSION FUNDS

The end goal of the entire pension fund management process depicted in Figure 3.1 is value creation. What is this value that pension fund stakeholders want their fiduciaries to create? Stakeholders should value two things on the asset side of DB pension plan balance sheets. The first is knowing that there are sufficient segregated assets backing the accrued pension promises. The second is knowing that the investment return on the assets helps fund the promised pension payments. The higher the asset returns, the lower the contribution rate required to deliver a predefined pension.

A knowledgeable, responsible board of governing fiduciaries knows there is usually a trade-off to be evaluated between the two deliverables of benefit security on the one hand, and high asset returns on the other. Such a board tackles that trade-off head-on and constructs funding and asset mix policies that best balance the financial interests of various classes of pension plan stakeholders.[4] These decision processes are examined further in Chapters 8 and 9.

Active management of fund assets is another potential source of additional return, and hence value creation for fund stakeholders. But whether to, and how to engage in the active management of all, or part of fund assets involves far more difficult, complex issues than most fund fiduciaries realize. Pension fund fiduciaries must be able to assess not only the efficiency of capital markets generally, but also the organizational ability of the fund's management to successfully exploit any available opportunities.

Because getting the right balance of passive and active, and internal and external investment management in the fund is so critical, it is logical that the fund's reward system should be tied to getting it right. This is all part of the subject matter of Chapters 10, 13, and 14. Finally, the map makes it obvious that all of the preceding information is just elegant theory unless value and its sources can actually be measured, both at the total fund level, and all the way down to the level of individual portfolios. Chapter 11 lays out a comprehensive, consistent value measurement framework.

A sage once remarked that saying is one thing, doing another. The following chapters test the map's usefulness in creating the excellent pension fund organization.

NOTES

1. The authors were founding partners of Pension Finance Associates Inc., a pension finance and investments advisory firm based in Toronto, Canada. They worked together from 1981 to 1984. Ambachtsheer's book *Pension*

Funds and the Bottom Line, (Homewood IL: Dow Jones-Irwin, 1986) drew heavily on the run-it-like-a-business consulting experience of the early 1980s. An important foundation of their consulting practice was a book written by Don Ezra in 1979, *Understanding Pension Fund Finance and Investments* (Toronto, ON: Pagurian Press, 1979).

2. The entire Summer 1995 issue of the *Journal of Applied Corporate Finance,* edited by Donald H. Chew and published by Stern Stewart Management Services, was devoted to recent studies in the field of organizational economics. Figure 3.1 was adapted from a schematic included in an article in that issue titled "The Economics of Organizational Architecture" by James Brickley, Clifford Smith, and Jerold Zimmerman. This article was also the source for the three cited principles of good organizational design.

3. The term used to describe the body of individuals that governs pension funds varies both within countries and between countries. "The board of trustees" is most frequently used by public sector pension funds in English-speaking countries. In the case of corporate funds in these countries, this body often goes by the name of "the pension committee of the board" or simply "the pension committee." As indicated in Chapter 1, note 5, we use the term governing fiduciaries to describe the pension fund governors, regardless of nationality or type of pension fund sponsor.

4. In the case of DC pension plans, governing fiduciaries don't have funding decisions to struggle with, as the plan contribution rate is predefined. However, some interesting questions arise if the combination of a given contribution rate and investment return are unlikely to produce the income replacement rates plan participants are targeting. The management of DC plans is the subject of Chapter 15.

PART TWO
WHAT EVERY PENSION FUND FIDUCIARY SHOULD KNOW ... OR HAVE A VIEW ON

There are certain things about pension law and economics that every fiduciary should know. Prudence, for example, is process. Another example is that pension payments are typically 80 percent funded by investment returns, and only 20 percent by contributions. However, it is net returns that fund pension payments, not gross returns. Thus garnering the benefits of economies of scale is critical to the success of the pension business.

No capital market in the world is perfectly efficient. Knowing this is not very useful, however. Which capital markets or market components are inefficient enough to make money in, and who can exploit such an opportunity? This is a much more useful question, but considerably more difficult to answer. Understanding the structure and the economics of the investment management industry is a precondition.

4

What Fiduciaries Should Know about Pension Law and Pension Economics

---

I'm overeducated in all the things I shouldn't have known at all.

—*Noel Coward*

SEVEN KEY PENSION ECONOMICS PRINCIPLES

This chapter is the first of three primers for governing fiduciaries. The scope here includes an overview of all the kinds of decisions and activities that pension systems involve. We also discuss the standards by which fiduciaries are judged and the fundamentals of pension fund economics. In doing this, we arrive at seven key principles that apply to every pension fund in every country: All governing fiduciaries should be familiar with them.

1. *Prudence is process.* Fiduciaries will be judged, not by a retrospective assessment of whether their decisions were successful, but by whether they followed a reasonable process in reaching their decisions.

2. *Know who your stakeholders are, and the true nature of the pension deal.* If you don't understand who has a legitimate interest in the fund's investment return, you can't make sensible decisions for them.

3. *Permit investment returns to pay for most of the benefits.* In the long term, they are far larger than contributions.

4. *No worthwhile opportunity comes without risk.* Thinking of return, or measuring return, without paying equal attention to the associated risk, is futile.

5. *The fund's asset allocation policy decision is, in practice, the most important investment decision.* Devote an appropriate amount of time to it.

6. *Economies of scale reduce operating costs.* And therefore increase returns net of costs. Few fiduciaries seek economies of scale.

7. *Define what the creation of investment value means to you.* A lack of courage in tackling this issue is the surest path to confusion and conflict later, when the time comes to evaluate the results.

PRUDENCE IS PROCESS

When fiduciaries perform their activities, by what standards will their behavior and decisions be judged?

We are not lawyers. We cannot, and do not, give legal advice. But our experience has enabled us to observe and listen to and read many discussions on fiduciary standards. Here is the essence of our understanding of the main issues involved.

In North America, most discussions start by referring to the most famous, and earliest, case on the subject, *Harvard College v. Amory,* in 1830. In his verdict, Justice Samuel Putnam made the now famous comment, "Do what you will, the capital is at hazard." By this he meant that no set of rules, no matter how detailed, could guarantee that an investment would turn out to be safe. The future is unpredictable. All that fiduciaries can do is exercise the best judgment available to them.

This is the foundation of the standard of prudence enunciated in pension law in the United States (the Employee Retirement Income Security

Act, commonly called ERISA). According to this act, a fiduciary must discharge his or her duties "with the care, skill, prudence, and diligence under the circumstances then prevailing that a prudent man acting in a like capacity and familiar with such matters would use in the conduct of an enterprise of a like character and with like aims."

The phrase "familiar with such matters" is usually interpreted as meaning that the fiduciary must be assumed to be knowledgeable. In particular, when advice from an expert is available, prudent trustees will avail themselves of this advice. In this sense, there is no excuse for failing to get expert input before decisions are made. Hence the standard is usually called the "prudent expert" standard.

Since the future is unpredictable, a decision made today, even with the best of advice and soundest of judgment may turn out poorly. This does not negate the prudence of the decision. Thus subsequent returns are not the basis by which prudence is judged. Instead, it is judged by the degree of care with which the decision was made. So fiduciaries have a duty to themselves, to document with care the considerations that guided any decision of theirs. Essentially, this means that the relevant facts and opinions must be considered as part of a process that is relevant to reaching the decision, and they must keep an adequate record of all this. Hence the snappy summing up of the standard: "Prudence is process."

Under ERISA, a fiduciary will be judged according to four tests, each of which will be applied in the context of the plan under consideration:

1. *Loyalty.* Decisions must be made solely in the interest of the participants and beneficiaries.
2. *Prudence.* The standard described earlier will be applied.
3. *Diversification.* The assets must be diversified to minimize the risk of large losses, unless the circumstances make it clearly prudent not to do so.
4. *Acting pursuant to plan documents.* Action must not be taken outside the scope permitted by these documents.

In addition, there are a number of absolute prohibitions, such as transactions between funds and their fiduciaries as suppliers of services (fiduciary self-dealing) that do not depend on the circumstances of the plan. Fiduciaries get legal advice on these matters. Little purpose is served in providing a checklist here.

In other countries, legal standards that apply to fiduciaries are broadly similar, but are stated differently.[1]

Fiduciaries need at all times to be able to answer "yes" to the following questions, and to demonstrate why they can confidently answer "yes":

- Have your decisions followed a reasonable process?
- Are your decisions sensible from the perspective of benefit security?
- Do you have a due diligence monitoring process to ensure that decisions made in the past are still appropriate today?
- Are the assets being managed in compliance with investment mandates?

It is a routine practice today for governing fiduciaries to receive compliance reports. It is not yet routine for them to authorize a procedural audit, questioning whether prudent procedures have not only been established, but are also being carried out. But this, too, is part of prudence.

KNOW WHO YOUR STAKEHOLDERS ARE, AND THE TRUE NATURE OF THE PENSION DEAL

What is the purpose of a pension fund?

There are two possible purposes:

1. The main, and sometimes the only, purpose is to be the primary source of security for benefits that are promised or intended. When pensions are backed by book reserves, or when the fund is in deficit (i.e., does not have enough money to meet the benefits), the sponsor may become the secondary source of security. A government agency may be a third source. But the fund's purpose is to provide security even if the sponsoring entity fails.

2. The other potential purpose, where it exists, is more subtle. If the sponsor has a direct economic interest in the fund's return, the opportunity to earn exceptional returns may itself be a part of the sponsor's purpose. Such a fund becomes a source of economic advantage to the sponsor.

Who then is affected by the fund's return?

There is a short answer and a long answer to this question. The short answer reflects the explicit direct relationship between the fund's benefits and the investment return. The long answer reflects highly controversial and difficult issues dealing with who looks at the return, how their actions are likely to be affected by the size of the return, and so on. Not surprisingly, many groups choose not to dwell on these issues.

A pension plan has a context. Part of that context is the written document that defines the plan, its benefits and contributions, and so on. That is where the direct connection between the fund's return and the plan's benefits is defined. But that is not the whole context. Other parts of the context are how the plan is communicated to employees, how it is administered, the history of the plan, and the total compensation package of which the plan forms a part. Sometimes the other parts contradict the written document. Then confusion arises, and it is important to clear up the nature of the pension deal. The lack of clarity may extend to confusion over who benefits when the investment return is high and who loses when it is low. This level of confusion is deadly, because unless you know who is the legitimate beneficiary of the investment return, it is not possible to decide on a sensible investment policy.[2]

The situation is not as inflamed today as it was, say, 10 years ago. Nevertheless, we can at least learn from history and identify some red flags:

- In times when inflation is high or increasing, protecting the purchasing power of benefits in a defined benefit plan can become an issue. The historical practice of augmenting benefits via ad hoc increases after pensions commenced was widespread. The increases were often financed by the higher expected returns that were anticipated to accompany higher inflation. This caused many groups of employees to feel entitled to a share of the investment return and the governance arrangements.

- When employees contribute to a defined benefit plan, they often take the view that their contributions are part of the capital base on which returns are earned, and they should explicitly receive some portion of higher-than-anticipated returns. Their feelings are held even more forcefully when the employer's contribution is stated not as "whatever it takes to provide the benefits," but as some stated contribution rate (as with some government plans). This is one aspect of the pension deal that would be easier to administer if it were faced explicitly and resolved. In one Canadian situation, for example, there is an explicit agreement to share both the surplus and the shortfall that can arise from investment returns. The agreement helps to define the deal, defines the interested parties in the investment return, defines value as the creation of investment surplus, sets the framework for discussing objectives and risk tolerance, and so on.[3]

- In some countries, there have been legal cases on the ownership of any surplus in a defined benefit plan. Courts tend to rule narrowly on the facts of a case, rather than on any underlying principles. In your own situation, ask: "Do all the fiduciaries, the sponsor, and the participants understand the ownership of the surplus?" If the answer is "no," the pension deal is not clear.

In defined contribution arrangements in most countries, the entire investment return is allocated to the active members of the pension plan. They are the most important stakeholders. But they are not the only stakeholders. Even though the sponsor may not participate directly in the return, the sponsor wants the pension plan to be successful. It is a waste of contributions if the fund fails to augment them with sufficiently high returns to provide good pensions. Count every contributor, whether sponsor or member, as a stakeholder.

We cannot overemphasize the importance of this issue. We elevate it to the level of a fundamental principle: Know who your stakeholders are, and the true nature of the pension deal.

At this point, we cannot avoid the apparent contradiction between the interests of all the stakeholders and ERISA's loyalty test. ERISA recognizes no constituency beyond the beneficiaries. We have emphasized that others have legitimate economic interests. Our experience suggests that, in practice, decisions are made with these other interests in mind—not to the exclusion of beneficiaries' interests, but in addition to them. When the interests are in conflict, the beneficiaries come first. When a decision can be made that reflects other interests without compromising the beneficiaries, then that decision can be implemented. It is a matter of judgment whether or not beneficiaries are compromised, but the size and economic legitimacy of other stakeholders' interests cannot be ignored in practice.

THE PENSION FUND BUSINESS AND ITS INVESTMENT FUNDAMENTALS

Whatever the pension deal, the governing fiduciaries must act as businesspeople. Their business is to deploy capital, which is provided to them in the form of contributions. Their goal is to create value for their stakeholders. What exactly constitutes value is the last issue we discuss in this chapter. Before we get there, we offer the next four principles as powerful summaries of pension fund economics.

Permit Investment Returns to Pay for Most of the Benefits

All pension funds work in the same way. This is summed up in what we call *the fundamental pension equation:*

Contributions + Investment returns = Benefits paid

This equation is familiar to all actuaries. Its wisdom is passed down from generation to generation as actuaries bounce their babies on their knees. Eventually everyone will understand its significance.

The right-hand side of the equation says that there is a need to accumulate wealth in the fund in order to pay benefits. The left-hand side of the equation says that there are only two ways to create wealth. One is to put money in. The other is to invest the money in the capital market and generate investment returns. In effect, the capital market becomes a generous, though capricious, third party (neither the employer nor the plan member) that augments the wealth of the fund.[4]

Depending on the economic climate, depending on the types of assets held, and depending on many other things, investment returns can turn out to be high or low, volatile, or relatively smooth. But they are always important, and they are always uncertain.

For a typical North American pension fund, in the long term roughly 20 percent of the wealth in a pension fund consists of contributions (whether made by the employer or the employees). The remaining 80 percent consist of the investment returns earned over time by the fund. Naturally, these are not precise numbers. In prolonged periods of high returns, the split may be closer to 90/10 in favor of investment returns. During prolonged periods of low returns, the split may be closer to 70/30 or even 60/40 in favor of investment returns. But as a rough rule of thumb, the 80/20 split is close enough. This is why it is so important to get as much wealth as possible created by the capital markets.

Figure 4.1 shows one set of calculations that illustrates this point.[5] Here's what is behind the calculations: Suppose there is only one plan member. For this member, contributions are made as a level percentage of salary for 30 years of service. Suppose this salary increases by 5 percent

	Contributions	Investment returns	
Preretirement	19¢	40¢	59¢
Postretirement	—	41¢	41¢
	19¢	81¢	100¢

FIGURE 4.1   Sources of Wealth in a Pension Fund.

each year. Suppose further that the pension fund earns an investment return of 8 percent per annum. When the member retires, the benefit is paid in the form of a level monthly pension, and continues for 15 years before death brings it to a close. Figure 4.1 illustrates this process:

- Of each dollar paid in benefits, 59 cents have been accumulated in the fund before retirement. The remaining 41 cents are earned on the balance in the fund as it is drawn down to pay the monthly benefits.
- Of each dollar paid in benefits, 19 cents are the sum total of the contributions. The remaining 81 cents are the sum total of the investment earnings.

Now many things become clear.

- The investment returns are typically much more important than contributions in building pension fund wealth. The main business that the trustees are involved in, therefore, is the business of generating investment returns.
- In a defined benefit plan, the cost of the benefits is essentially determined by the level of investment returns. Contributions are virtually a residual: they are whatever the capital markets do not pay for. A sponsor can only have an acceptable level of contributions if the fund earns an acceptable level of investment returns.
- Paying benefits in the form of a lump sum on retirement rather than as regular monthly payments has serious investment consequences. The onus for earning the final 41 cents in each dollar of benefits is placed squarely on the shoulders of the recipient of the lump sum. What the recipient does with the money is, to put it mildly, a nontrivial question.
- In a defined contribution plan under which members make their own asset allocation decisions, educating them so that they actually put the contributions to work effectively is all-important. Without sensible decisions, it is very likely that the 19 cents of contributions shown in Figure 4.1 will earn very much less than their

fair 81 cents of investment return, and thus defeat the benefits policy that the plan is meant to implement. More on this in Chapter 13
on defined contribution plans.

The 81/19 calculations are based on a pension fund that gets its investment returns free of tax. If a fund is taxed, the relevant returns are
net-of-tax returns. Each 19 cents of contributions will ultimately generate less than 81 cents of net investment return. If the tax rate is, say, 15
percent, and the gross return averages, say, 8 percent per annum, the net
rate will average 6.8 percent per annum. Over the lifetime of a participant, this will reduce the 81 cents of investment return to perhaps 58
cents. When this is compared with 19 cents of contributions, the proportion of the total arising from net investment returns is then 75 percent
and from contributions 25 percent.

No Worthwhile Opportunity Comes without Risk

No investment can shelter the investor from every kind of risk. The governing fiduciaries must realize, therefore, that their investment decisions will not be "right" or "wrong." Rather, their decisions will always
be based on weighing different kinds of risks, and different kinds of opportunities, and will reflect the balance of risks and opportunities where
they are most comfortable. Figure 4.2 illustrates this point.

All investments have two desirable characteristics: safety and opportunity. These qualities are at opposite ends of the investment spectrum.

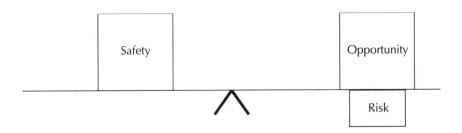

FIGURE 4.2   Investment Principle: Returns Come with Risks.

Along with opportunity comes risk. Asset classes are available throughout the spectrum. How one mixes the asset classes is called "asset allocation," and it essentially reflects where one wants to position oneself in the safety versus opportunity-with-risk spectrum. Not surprisingly, this is the single most important investment decision anyone can make. We will discuss the relevant considerations in Chapter 9.

A little thought will confirm that safety and opportunity for high returns should not simultaneously characterize a single investment. Suppose that an investment does have both: It is safe (meaning there is little chance of its price declining) and it has a very high expected return. In an efficient market (meaning one where information about investments is widely disseminated, and the cost of buying and selling investments is small), investors would flock to such an investment. They would bid its price up as they fight to buy it. At the higher price, its expected return becomes lower, and it is no longer as safe. It would still be desirable, and its price would keep being bid up, until its combination of relative opportunity and relative risk are in rough equilibrium with other available investments. Thus, in reasonably efficient markets, obtaining higher expected returns requires taking higher risks.[6]

This is not just theory. It happens in practice. Figure 4.3 shows the average annual returns for three well-researched and easily acquired asset classes in the United States: Treasury bills, bonds, and stocks. It is immediately apparent that the steadiest investment has had the lowest average return, and the most volatile investment has had the highest average return.

We have taken some trouble to explain this principle, because in our experience it is where governing fiduciaries' difficulties with investment decisions first reveal themselves. They want safety and opportunity at the same time. And it is not only governing fiduciaries who want high returns but are reluctant to acknowledge that they have to accept commensurate risks of potentially bad outcomes. Even wealthy businesspeople who otherwise would seem to be sophisticated investors, behave this way. In a newspaper interview, Amy Elliott, a Citicorp private banker, reflected on the subject of Raul Salinas de Gortari, brother of Carlos Salinas de Gortari, Mexico's president from 1988 to 1994. Raul Salinas invested over $80 million with Citibank.[7]

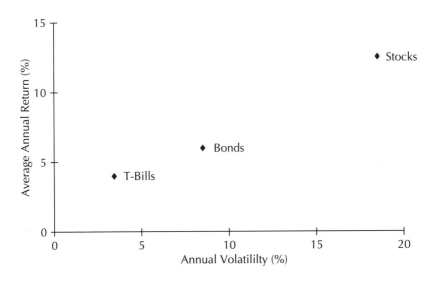

FIGURE 4.3   Investment Risks and Rewards in the United States, 1920–1996.

She said she had to school Mr. Salinas in the tradeoff between risk and reward. A "medium-sophistication-level" investor, he was eager to get returns of 13 percent to 15 percent, but then was unwilling to take the risks needed to get such returns. She scaled back his expectations to "low two digits." They decided on a global-bond portfolio, she said.

In a pension fund context, a portfolio of global bonds, without other asset classes to diversify it, would be considered a very risky investment.

At this early stage, we have oversimplified the presentation a little. As we will see in Chapter 9, volatility of return is only one aspect of risk. Risk itself is a broader concept. And, in any event, risk is best established in the context of the liabilities that are being funded. What is safe for a defined benefit plan is not the same as what is safe for a defined contribution plan. Moreover, while we have used the issue of asset allocation policy to illustrate that risks are attached to every worthwhile opportunity, the same is true of virtually every investment issue. For example, active management offers the opportunity to outperform market benchmarks. But it also carries the risk of underperformance.

The Fund's Asset Allocation Policy Decision Is, in Practice, the Most Important Investment Decision

Of all the decisions and activities, which have the greatest impact on achieving the fund's objectives? There are two ways to look at this:

1. *The legal perspective.* Knowing the status of the fund and its benefits is essential to being a prudent fiduciary. The compilation of reports to be reviewed can be delegated to others by the governing fiduciaries. The responsibility to review them cannot.

2. *The financial perspective.* Here we are talking about the creation and management of the fund's wealth. The portion of the wealth that consists of contributions made to the fund is typically beyond the control of the fiduciaries. Hence our focus here is on the fund's investment returns.

A number of studies explain what most affects a fund's returns.[8] Their details are fascinating to those who love empirical analyses. For fiduciaries, the lessons can be summed up simply. Table 4.1 shows the relative importance of the many kinds of investment decisions that are made for a pension fund, and the frequency with which the decision makers reassess their current attitudes or holdings.

Most defined benefit funds adopt some long-term asset allocation policy. This represents the trade-off between seeking opportunity and seeking safety that feels most comfortable to the decision makers, given the characteristics of their liabilities, what they hope to achieve, and the state of the capital markets. There is no need to change this policy unless the liabilities, objectives, risk tolerance, or market prospects change noticeably—which typically does not happen for several years. Nevertheless, current practice is moving toward periodic reviews as frequently as every year.

Interestingly, most defined benefit funds in any country have similar asset allocation policies. In other words, if one were to construct the average of everyone's asset allocation policies, most funds would be similar to this average, though most funds would also be a little bit different

Table 4.1   The Relative Importance of Different Investment Decisions

Type of Decision	Typical Review Frequency	Typical Importance

A. Long-term asset allocation policy:
  1. What are capital market prospects?
  2. What is our lowest-risk posture?
  3. What are our competitors doing?
  4. What characteristics of our own situation
    justify our being different?
	1–3 years	High

B. Short-term tactical departures from asset allocation policy	Daily/Often	Moderate

C. Implementation strategy:
  1. Active or passive.
  2. Style preferences or neutrality.
  3. Balanced or specialist mandates.
  4. Securities or direct investments.
	Market cycle	Moderate

D. Manager—selection/retention/replacement:
  1. Internal or external.
  2. Compensation arrangements.
	Market cycle	Moderate

E. Security selection	Daily/Often	Moderate

from the national average. In Table 4.1, the ultimate decision on long-term policy is Decision A.

Some funds employ investment management professionals who believe that capital markets are not always in equilibrium: Asset classes are temporarily mispriced relative to each other, and these mispricings can be exploited in the short term by making brief tactical departures (monitored daily and sometimes almost continuously) from the long-term policy. These constitute Decision B in Table 4.1.

Most funds also have each of their asset classes invested similarly. In other words, if we were to take the average holdings in any asset class, most funds would own a list of holdings in that asset class that is broadly similar to the average, though most funds would also be a little bit different from the average. This, too, is part of diversification. But funds arrive at their asset class holdings through a succession of decisions.

Should we consciously hold the average (be passive), or attempt to take advantage of relative mispricings that occur within asset classes (be active)? If we decide to be active, should we persistently favor one subset of the asset class (a style preference) or be neutral in this regard? If we hire investment management professionals to be active, should we give them specialist asset class mandates or should they have wide-ranging mandates? Should we invest in liquid securities or hold direct investments, too? All these involve issues of manager structure, and belong to Decision C in Table 4.1. These are not decisions that can be evaluated daily. Whether they work in the fund's favor requires at least one up-cycle in the asset class and one down-cycle, for a fair evaluation. A complete market cycle (however long that may turn out to be) is therefore the minimum time period for which these decisions tend to be kept in place.

The actual selection of managers, whether internal or external, is Decision D, again typically requiring a complete market cycle as a minimum for a fair evaluation. The actual selection of securities by managers is Decision E, obviously under continuous review. We have added something under Decision D that typically is ignored: how to compensate investment managers. We will look at this again in later chapters.

So much for background. Now to the results of the empirical analyses.

Decision A, resulting in the fund's asset allocation policy, has by far the greatest impact on the long-term pattern of the fund's returns. This is the primary investment decision. All other decisions are secondary. This does not mean that the other decisions cannot be as important as the primary decision. That depends on how large a difference from the average position the fiduciaries are prepared to contemplate in the secondary Decisions B through E. The studies simply observe that, for most funds, typical differences in Decisions B through E have much less impact than the primary asset allocation policy decision. The order of magnitude stated is that the primary decision has about 10 times the combined impact of the four secondary decisions, in a typical case.

Hence the principle that the asset allocation policy decision is, in practice, the most important investment decision.

Most North American corporate and union defined benefit funds have already exploited this principle to its fullest extent, in the sense that they already have asset allocation policies that push their risk tolerance to its limit. This is also true in other countries, such as the United Kingdom. But in many government defined benefit funds, as well as all types of defined contribution arrangements, asset allocation policies appear so risk-averse that they leave large amounts of potential return unclaimed. Perhaps the answer is fiduciary and stakeholder education.

Economies of Scale Reduce Unit Operating Costs

In almost every aspect of business, there are economies of scale. The more one can assemble identical actions or decisions, the less it costs to make them (up to a point, at any rate). The same holds true for the costs of pension fund investing and administration.

A 1996 study quantified the impact of size on operating costs.[9]

The operating costs of 262 funds in North America were carefully assembled. These costs included those at the governing, managing, and operating levels. Four factors explained most of the difference between the costs of the participating funds. Three of these factors are not surprising. Funds with greater exposure to assets in privately traded markets (such as real estate) incurred higher costs. Funds with greater exposure to equities incurred higher costs. And, mainly because of the fees charged for active investment management, Canadian funds incurred lower costs than American funds.

But the factor with by far the biggest explanatory power on costs was fund size. Across all sizes of funds, a 10-fold increase in asset size reduced annual operating costs (per dollar of assets, or unit costs) by roughly 20 basis points a year, other things (such as asset allocation) being equal.

Moreover, since the study found no significant difference between the gross (that is, preexpense) fund returns when ranked by size (other things being equal, such as asset allocation), the reduction in unit costs associated with size appears to be pure gravy. It simply increases the return, net of costs, by roughly 20 basis points each year for every 10-fold increase in size.

A similar dynamic is at work in benefits administration.[10] And increasingly, sponsors of pension plans are outsourcing their benefits record keeping to take advantage of the cost savings. Investment cost savings have long been obtained across the pension funds of a common sponsor: That's why master trusts were started. But the logical extension to pooling the assets of the pension funds of several sponsors, to obtain really large investment cost savings, has not yet become widely popular.[11]

DEFINE WHAT THE CREATION OF INVESTMENT VALUE MEANS TO YOU

What is an adequate investment return?

Many governing fiduciaries behave as if the words "adequate" and "competitive" are interchangeable. Their first focus is invariably to compare their returns with those earned by a sample of other funds. There is a straightforward logic that easily justifies this attitude.

For example, consider a defined benefit pension fund. What is the purpose of the pension plan itself? For a typical sponsor, the plan's genesis probably lies in the notion of a competitive total compensation package, of which a retirement benefit plan is an important component. Thus the stated purpose of the plan may be to provide benefits at the median level of firms in the same industry. For such a sponsor, a corollary might be to provide the benefit at a competitive cost. This implies that the fund must earn a competitive return. Investment value might then be defined as earning this return at a lower-than-average cost. Or it might be defined as earning a higher than simply competitive return, without taking more investment risk than the competition.

That is one possible starting point. But the starting point is merely a device for looking at the fundamental issues. Ultimately, considerations about the creation of investment value involve three aspects. What was the achieved return? Did it justify taking the risks involved? Did it justify the investment costs involved? If you can say, "My fund earned a return that more than compensated for the risks and costs involved," you have, without a doubt, witnessed the creation of investment value.

Alignment on the definition of what constitutes the creation of investment value is the single most important aspect of the decision makers' responsibilities. A lack of courage, or knowledge, at this stage is the surest path to confusion and conflict later, when the time comes to evaluate the results. Don't leave implicit the things that ought to be explicit.

In Chapter 11, we take the notion of creating investment value to a logical and measurable definition.

NOTES

1. For example, see Sections 22(1) and 22(2) of The Ontario Pension Benefits Act (Revised Statutes of Ontario, 1990) for the standards in one Canadian province. These are broadly similar to the treatment in other Canadian jurisdictions. See also, *The Trustee Guidebook to Superannuation*, published by the Insurance and Superannuation Commission of Australia (Melbourne, 1996) for the Australian perspective.

2. A more complete treatment of the subject is contained in "Whose Pension Fund?" by D. Don Ezra, *Canadian Investment Review*, Vol. I, No. 1, Fall 1988. That article is itself condensed from *The Nature of the Pension Agreement*, published as Research Report No. 1 by Ontario's Task Force on the Investment of Public Sector Pension Funds, Ontario Government Bookstore, Toronto, 1987.

3. This is the approach adopted by the Ontario Teachers' Pension Plan, featured in Chapter 13.

4. Some commentators rightly point out that the wealth created on the left-hand side of the equation must be sufficient not only to pay the benefits but also all expenses involved in operating the pension system. They then expand the right-hand side to say: benefits paid + expenses. For our purposes, while their revision is correct, in most cases expenses are tiny relative to benefits paid, and so we will use the simpler form of the equation.

5. For a more complete treatment of the subject, see the article from which the example is taken: "A Model of Pension Fund Growth" by Don Ezra, Russell Research Commentary, 1989.

6. For an outstandingly readable version of the story of capital market concepts and the people responsible for them, including many Nobel laureates, see *Capital Ideas* by Peter L. Bernstein, (New York: The Free Press, 1992).

7. "Private banker wooed, then sought to drop Mexico's Raul Salinas" by Laurie Hays, *Wall Street Journal*, November 1, 1996.

8. The seminal paper on the subject is "Determinants of Portfolio Performance" by Gary Brinson, L. Randolph Hood, and Gilbert L. Beebower, *Financial Analysts Journal*, July–August 1986. This study was updated in "Determinants of Portfolio Performance II: An Update" by Gary

Brinson, B. D. Singer, and Gilbert L. Beebower, *Financial Analysts Journal,* May–June 1991. Since the conclusions of these studies are so often misunderstood and misquoted, a third paper, "The Importance of the Asset Allocation Decision" by Chris R. Hensel, D. Don Ezra, and John H. Ilkiw, *Financial Analysts Journal,* July–August 1991, attempted to clarify the main sources of the level of a fund's returns in the long term, and the shape of the return curve.

9. For complete details, see the 1996 study by Cost Effectiveness Measurement Inc., Toronto. Referenced in Chapter 2, note 5.

10. Peter Skinner of ComSuper, in "International Best Practice in Superannuation Administration" (SES Fellowship Report, Canberra, Australia, 1997) shows that many of the principles and practices on the asset side have counterparts on the benefits side.

11. The closest examples of asset pooling across multiple plan sponsors at this time are probably the Dutch and Australian industry funds.

5

What Fiduciaries Should Know about Capital Markets

Those who are enamoured of practice without science are like a pilot who goes into a ship without a rudder or compass and never has any certainty where he is going. Practice should always be based upon a sound knowledge of theory.

—*Leonardo da Vinci*

FIVE KEY CAPITAL MARKETS PRINCIPLES

In Chapter 4, we identified seven key principles for governing fiduciaries in connection with fiduciary standards and pension economics. This chapter presents five principles for managing fiduciaries in connection with capital markets. Governing fiduciaries need to understand these principles, too, or they will not be in a position to evaluate their managing fiduciaries. And, in practice, operating fiduciaries are not always familiar with the effect of the following principles on how they are hired, evaluated and, alas, sometimes terminated:

1. *All investment markets are inefficient.* This is simply a more dramatic way of saying that no market is perfectly efficient: all are,

to a greater or lesser extent, inefficient. Inefficiency creates opportunities to outperform others. It also hinders the capture of superior returns. You need to have supportable views on the degrees and types of inefficiency in different markets.

2. *Investment markets are composed of segments.* Asset classes do not move in perfect correlation with each other. To a lesser extent, securities within an asset class also break up into different return patterns. You need to be aware of the segments (often called "styles") within the asset classes that you are dealing with.

3. *Active management involves both investment and human processes.* You need to understand both. They are often difficult to describe.

4. *There is an optimal size for a manager's assets under management.* A larger asset base facilitates research. But at some stage, larger trading block sizes create market impacts large enough to negate the value of the research. You need to have a supportable view on whether your managers have passed their optimal sizes.

5. *Charge investment returns with the direct cost of management and the indirect cost of risk taken.* Investors understand the difference between returns that are gross and net of investment management fees and other costs. They rarely assess a charge for risk exposure. You can be misled if you do not consider the opportunity cost of undertaking risk in a different, perhaps more rewarding, way.

All Investment Markets Are Inefficient

What is an efficient market? One in which security prices reflect all available information.

For such a market to exist, information must be generated constantly, flow rapidly, and be easily accessible to all who want it. Market participants must agree on the significance of new information. And it must be easy for security transactions to take place quickly and inexpensively, so that new prices can reflect the implications of the new information.

In such a market, all securities are fairly priced, and the only way to earn a superior return consistently is to take on commensurately higher risk. If one portfolio outperforms another with the same level of risk, it must be due to luck. Any textbook on investing will provide references to evidence that no market is completely efficient.[1] There are two types of inefficiency. One is the friend of active management; the other is its enemy.

The friendly form of inefficiency is informational inefficiency. Information may not be easily available. This is true of data on emerging markets or real estate transactions, or even in the average gap between corporate fiscal year-ends and the arrival of financial statements at the Institutional Brokers' Estimate System (IBES). Or information comes in unfamiliar forms, (e.g., different accounting conventions in different countries). Or it is not interpreted in the same way by all analysts, as evidenced by different forecasts of corporate earnings, interest rate movements, or currency movements.

The inimical form of inefficiency is that prices may not reflect the available information. Partly, this is because of transaction costs, which limit the extent to which it is worthwhile to trade on new information. Such costs include commissions, taxes and fees on trades, and the bid-offer spread. Then there is the active management fee, which may be considered a proxy for a pension fund's cost of acquiring information. The degree of illiquidity in a market, and the degree of concentration of holdings, may be other impediments to prices fully reflecting available information.

Ideally, it would be possible to plot all capital markets on a two-dimensional grid, as in Figure 5.1.[2] One dimension would measure the informational inefficiency in the market, combining measures of the examples cited earlier. The other dimension would measure the cost of capturing information in security prices, again combining measures of the examples cited. The purpose of such a grid would be to identify the relative inefficiency of different capital markets. The greater the inefficiency, the greater the chance of earning superior returns in that market, though at the cost of added risk and active management fees. Managing fiduciaries need to assess different markets to decide where they have the greatest chance of creating value by active management.

So: what might become apparent by completing Figure 5.1?

The most inefficient markets are those called "privately traded": real estate, private placements of equity and debt, partnership funds, and so

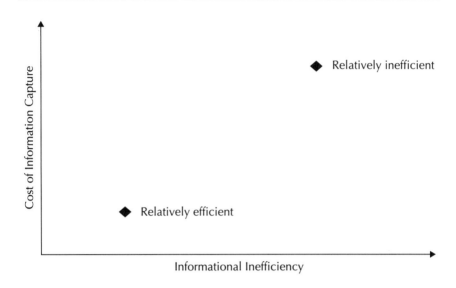

FIGURE 5.1   Are Markets Efficient?

on. Each of these is different, so research is extremely labor-intensive and vehicle-specific. This makes for sparse, expensive research. The instruments are closely held, so liquidity is virtually nonexistent. They are thinly traded, if traded at all, so values must be appraised rather than set by trading. Most funds avoid these instruments, because it costs so much in time and money to acquire a working familiarity with them at the fiduciaries' level, though the opportunities to make (or lose) money are undeniable. The notable exception is real estate, which has long found a home in defined benefit funds around the world.

Next, in order of inefficiency, are markets that are publicly but thinly traded. Emerging market equity and debt would fall under this heading. Following them would be small developed markets, such as the smaller European countries.

Larger markets show some differences. Continental Europe and Japan are relatively inefficient in providing user-friendly information, while the cost of capture may be relatively small because of market size. In contrast, Australian and Canadian culture makes their markets more informationally efficient, but the cost of information capture may be relatively high. Finally, the U.S. markets are probably the most efficient in both senses.

Within countries, there would be some differences too. Equity markets are generally more efficient than corporate debt markets but less efficient than sovereign debt markets. Within equities, larger companies are more efficiently researched and traded than smaller companies.

Are markets becoming more efficient as time passes? Many people believe so. A simple pragmatic test is to look at studies of the relative performance of active managers in a particular asset class or style. Measure the difference between the upper and lower quartile breaks—the range of returns that captures the middle 50 percent of the managers (ignore the extreme returns, which often reflect one-shot instances of good or bad luck). If a market is becoming more efficient, that interquartile range should be declining over time. Conversely, if the range is not declining, efficiency does not seem to be increasing.

Table 5.1, which is one variant on such a test, seems to indicate a slight increase in the efficiency of the markets shown over time, except for the growth equity portion of the U.S. market.

Investment Markets Are Composed of Segments

What is an asset class? It is a definition of convenience, not of precision. An asset class is a group of investments that, either conceptually or because of return patterns, one tends to think of as relatively homogeneous. Asset classes do not move in perfect correlation with each other.

Table 5.1 Difference between Quartile Breaks for Active Management, Asset Classes, and Styles in the United States

Years	Value Equities	Growth Equities	Market-Oriented Equities	Fixed Income
1981–1985	8.4%	7.3%	7.5%	5.9%
1986–1990	7.5	6.5	6.2	3.4
1991–1995	6.4	8.5	6.1	3.5

Source: Frank Russell Company, Russell Performance Universe System.

Recognizing this, one can take advantage of the differences in their return patterns to reduce risk by diversification.

To a lesser extent, securities within an asset class also break up into different return patterns. You need to be aware of the segments (often called "styles") within the asset classes that you are dealing with. This is a concept American investors are very familiar with. In other countries, investors are either unfamiliar with or skeptical of the concept.

If you are not American, you may shake your head in amazement at the degree of specialization to be found among U.S. equity managers. Surely, you say, managers in my country don't invest that way. My country doesn't have growth and value managers: they're all simply "market-oriented," aren't they? Because even if they wanted to specialize, our domestic equity market isn't nearly broad enough to permit such specialization. Nor is it deep enough for a manager to make a living by focusing on only one part of it. And in any event, I don't see that "style universes" (presentations of the results of managers with the same style) are prevalent. So none of that applies to me—thank goodness!

Think again.

Whether managers behave in stylistic ways isn't relevant. The real issue is whether style portfolios perform differently. If they do, then managing fiduciaries have the capability for better risk control. This is simply derived from the argument for asset classes. Whether managers specialize in different asset classes doesn't matter. All that matters is whether different asset classes perform differently. And they do. That gives governing fiduciaries the capability to control their fund's total risk exposure, by specifying the asset allocation policy they want. So too with styles, which are nothing more than subsets of asset classes, just as asset classes are nothing more than subsets of all available investments.

The difference between the annual returns of the value and growth subsets of domestic equity markets is more volatile in France, Japan, the United Kingdom, Germany, and Switzerland than in the United States.[3] Given these findings, the amazing thing is not that significant differences between value and growth exist in the other countries. It is that the effect was first noticed in the United States, where the differences are smallest.

Yes, styles do exist in other countries. That means managing fiduciaries need to know whether their managers are indeed core broad-market-oriented managers. And they need to take care to structure their exposure to each asset class in a balanced way, not in a way restricted to just one style or segment (see Chapter 10, the section "The Best Managing Fiduciaries in Action").

Active Management Involves Both Investment and Human Processes

Ask anyone who has worked with investment managers and research analysts, and you are bound to get this uniform response: They are very smart people. It is the first thing you notice about them. They are well educated, knowledgeable about their field, and . . . just plain smart. And they love their work. It's almost a pity that some of them are, by definition, bound to produce below-average performance. But they don't stay below average for long. Everyone has a period of above-average performance to show. Choosing between them isn't a simple matter.

A second characteristic of the group of managers and analysts may take longer to recognize, but it's there to see once you look for it. They view the world in different ways. They interpret information in different ways. They select securities in different ways and for different reasons. Never mind what you hear about the herd instinct, it doesn't show up in their portfolios. That's why their returns are different. It is difficult to explain the precise differences in the ways in which they acquire, process and evaluate information, and construct portfolios on the basis of their evaluation. Yet this turns out to be the only way to distinguish between them in advance.

Identifying winners after the fact is easy. No other profession has its results so often measured and published. But when you hire a manager, you buy future performance, not past performance. And to predict the future, you can't rely solely on past performance. Numerous studies have moved this suspicion to a confident assertion.[4] That means you have to go beyond the numbers.

Essentially, an investment management firm produces one or more products. The essential ingredient of each product is judgment. It is an invisible ingredient. It is concealed in the portfolios assembled by the firm, and only by studying the portfolios can one reach an informed opinion about the process of judgment that went into it. The factory in which judgments are produced is also impossible to see. It consists of the minds of all those involved in the process: each mind separately, as well as the interaction of the minds together. Some active management processes are, very subjective and intuitive. Others, though they are highly quantitative, no less contain a fundamentally subjective element in the design of the quantitative approach used.

You might think that it should be easy to ask a firm what process it uses to form judgments, and get a definitive answer, but it isn't. Experience shows that it is very difficult to describe every aspect of the process. Managers are often unconscious of some aspects. Sometimes, too, their process works in ways that are different from their descriptions of it, and they are not conscious of those differences. And their process changes gradually over time, though often so subtly that it is difficult to realize the cumulative effect.[5] Truly, the human mind is complex. And when it is the factory that one can only observe from the outside, forming a judgment about which group of factories will produce the best performance can be very difficult indeed.

Because historical performance alone is an unreliable predictor, one turns to other approaches. The most promising avenue appears to be the study of "the four Ps": people, process, portfolios, and performance.

Who are the people involved in performing research and translating it into judgments? What is their intellectual background, what is their experience, how long have they held their current roles?

Look at two aspects of their process. The first is the investment aspect. What is the idea that they believe will result in superior performance? How do they gather research to support it? How do they go about putting it into practice? The second is the human aspect. What are the dynamics of the decision makers? How much does each influence the final judgment? Is the firm really a single group or a collection of talented individuals with their own ideas? Many a good idea fails to be implemented well because of friction, or lack of courage or leadership, in relationships. As people come and go in the firm, the people dynamics inevitably change. Indeed, that is often why the process changes. These aspects are difficult to capture in a written description, and managers themselves are often not the best suppliers of such a description.

From the study of the people and the investment and human processes being applied, a shrewd analyst should be able to form expectations of the characteristics of the portfolios that the firm will hold. Not the actual holdings, of course: These will vary over time. But certain characteristics should remain stable. In some cases, certain characteristics will be predictably volatile. The type of characteristic that is relevant may be, for example, the price/earnings (P/E) ratio of a domestic equity portfolio relative to the entire equity market, the length of a domestic bond portfolio relative to the entire market, or the degree of country concentration in a global equity or bond portfolio. A comparison of the actual characteristics of the portfolios held in the past with the expected characteristics is very revealing. It might indicate that the process description is simply inconsistent with the way the manager has behaved in the past. Or that at present, the manager is holding a portfolio with most unusual characteristics. Or that the manager adheres faithfully to the process, through good times and bad.

Finally, in addition to the portfolio analysis, the historical performance should be consistent with the pattern of performance that other managers with similar approaches have achieved.

Nothing can directly predict whether the manager will do well or poorly, relative to others with a similar approach, in the future. The best one can say is that one thoroughly understands the manager. The relative performance prediction is itself a judgment made by the managing fiduciaries after a study of a wide range of managers.

There Is an Optimal Size for a Manager's Assets under Management

In a way, the size of the assets managed by a particular investment firm is a measure of the confidence that investors have in that firm. But size can have a negative effect on investment performance. As assets under management grow, so do the block sizes in which the manager's trades take place. Larger block sizes tend to increase the spread between the bid and asked prices. This "market impact" hurts the ability of the manager to realize the value of the research that prompts the trade. As block size increases, at some stage the market impact is large enough to make it pointless to trade further in that security, because the trade will actually cause money to be lost. Then the portfolio suffers an opportunity cost, because the value of the research cannot be realized.

One way to measure the combined effect of execution and opportunity costs is to compare the performance of an actual portfolio with the performance of the firm's ideal "paper" portfolio; that is, a portfolio that reflects all desired trades, executed at current prices. The difference between the performances of these two portfolios is the "implementation shortfall": a useful concept. It equals the sum of execution and opportunity costs actually incurred.

The effect of more assets under management is to increase the implementation shortfall. Transaction costs on executed orders are higher, and opportunity costs increase as a growing number of orders go unexecuted. The greater the implementation shortfall, the worse the performance of the actual portfolio.

What lessons does this simple concept provide?

First, there is, in principle, an optimal size for a manager's assets under management. In practice, the optimal size will depend on the quality of the manager's research, the manager's transaction needs, and the depth of the market (because in a deep market, the impact of a trade on price will rise slowly rather than fast, as block size increases). The optimal size for one investment process may be quite inappropriate for another. Calculations by Perold and Salomon, however, imply a surprisingly low optimal size.[6] For example, with research worth an additional 3 percent per annum relative to a passive benchmark, and market depth such that a $20 million block has a 3 percent spread differential relative to a small trade, the asset size after which no further wealth can be created is roughly $1 billion.

Second, the concept of implementation shortfall suggests a fee structure that aligns the manager's interest with the client's interest. The client has no interest in seeing the manager's assets expand beyond the optimal size. Yet, if the management fee is a fixed percentage of assets, the manager has a direct interest in increasing assets. The usual fee structure that declines with the account size exacerbates this divergence of interests.

One way of aligning the interests is to make the manager's fee a share of the dollar wealth added (that is, the dollars of return over and above what a benchmark return would have produced). Then the manager cannot gain by expanding beyond the optimal size. It is necessary for all the firm's clients to act in this way, or the manager will still have an incentive to grow beyond the optimal size. Client ownership of a portion of the firm or its revenue stream is a potential solution to this problem.

These are difficult issues to resolve. But the best managing fiduciaries will at least be aware of these principles, and strive to use them in practice.

Charge Investment Returns with the Direct Cost of Management and the Indirect Cost of Risk Taken

Investors understand the difference between returns that are gross and net of investment management fees. They rarely assess a charge for risk exposure. You can be misled if you do not consider the opportunity cost of undertaking risk in a different, perhaps more rewarding, way.

The tradition in measuring the investment performance of pension funds has been to calculate gross returns, that is, returns before deducting investment management fees. The original reason for this practice is that fiduciaries wanted to compare the performance of managers. However, the fund accumulates net of those fees, so the returns also need to be measured on a net basis.

Many boards look at these issues. They are relatively easy to investigate. But the subject should not end there. Risk exposure itself is pointless unless it receives a reward. So it is necessary to consider how much risk is being taken, and what is reasonable compensation for it. What is reasonable depends on the other risky opportunities the sponsor might have pursued.

For example, instead of adopting a risky asset allocation policy in the pension fund, the sponsor might prefer to take little risk in the fund and more risk in whatever is the main business of the sponsor. In this case, an appropriate charge for the asset allocation policy risk would be the return the sponsor might have expected from taking the same amount of risk in the main business.

As another example, most pension funds are actively managed. The risk involved here is often called nonmarket risk. Fiduciaries realize that the market, *as a whole,* provides no reward—ever—for taking on nonmarket risk. To earn a reward here, you have to beat the rest of the market. But as observed in Chapter 2, the risk exposure itself requires compensation. The sponsor, again, might have preferred to take the equivalent risk in the main business. Or perhaps the reward would have been greater if, instead of taking nonmarket risk, the asset allocation policy had been riskier. What would have been the rewards from those alternative forms of risk exposure? Those rewards are possible measures of the charge that should be assessed for taking nonmarket risk.

These are difficult calculations to perform.[7] But the principle is simple. When you take on risks, it is not enough to break even. You ought to be compensated for the risks you take. If you receive the same compensation for taking your risks that someone else could reasonably have earned, then you have administered the fund well, but you have not necessarily invested it excellently. Excellence lies in getting a higher return than implied by reasonable compensation for risk. Then it is clearly you who have added value. Indeed, you have *created* value for the fund.

NOTES

1. Two texts that cover a broad range of topics from a number of perspectives, and succeed in being both educational and readable, are *Managing Investment Portfolios: A Dynamic Process* (2nd ed.), edited by John L. Maginn and Donald L. Tuttle (Charlottesville, VA: The Association for Investment Management Research, 1990) and *Readings in Investment,* edited by Stephen Lofthouse (Chichester, England: John Wiley & Sons, 1994).

2. We are grateful to Stephen E. Wiltshire, Jon A. Christopherson, and Ann T. Skala of Frank Russell Company for the ideas and examples in this section of the chapter.

3. See "International Value and Growth Stock Returns" by Carlo Capaul, Ian Rowley, and William F. Sharpe, *Financial Analysts Journal,* January/February 1993. They divided each domestic equity market into value and growth components by the same rule that is typically used in the United States, and then measured return differences between January 1981 and May 1992. Corroborating evidence is found in studies by BARRA, Parametric, IFC, and Baring International.

4. See "Does Historical Performance Predict Future Performance?" by Ronald N. Kahn and Andrew Rudd, *Financial Analysts Journal,* November/December 1995, and "On Persistence in Mutual Fund Performance" by Mark Carhart, *Journal of Finance,* March 1997.

5. How many quarters does it take before the performance of a "top quartile" manager is statistically significant at the 95 percent level of confidence? It varies from country to country and from asset class to asset class. In the United States, the average top-quartile manager over the five years 1992–1996 required roughly 50 quarters before the performance reached that level of statistical significance. And how long before the bottom-quartile managers have such poor performance that their negative value added has the same level of significance? Typically 1,500 quarters! Why such a long time? Because the underperformance of these managers is overwhelmed by the volatility of their tracking error.

    However, even though it takes long observation to detect skill when statistical techniques are the only tool used, managers change their approach before the required track records can be established. A survey of 10 large equity and 10 large fixed-income managers conducted in 1997 was reported in an unpublished paper by George D. Oberhofer of Frank Russell Company. Over the previous five years, the investment process itself was changed in an important way (changing the philosophy, the security screening system used, the index to which the product was benchmarked, etc.) an average of 12 times per fixed-income manager and 5 times per equity manager. An average of six senior staff changes took place. And ownership of the firm changed, on average, slightly more than once for each firm surveyed. The mental factory from which performance is the output was by no means the same at the end of the five years as it had been at the start.

6. The discussion in this section is based on "The Right Amount of Assets under Management" by André F. Perold and Robert S. Salomon, Jr., *Financial Analysts Journal,* May/June 1991.

7. See Chapter 11 for further discussion on how risk-adjusted net value-added (RANVA) can be estimated.

6

What Fiduciaries Should Know about the Investment Management Services Market

---

But then one is always excited by descriptions of money changing hands. It's much more fundamental than sex.

—Nigel Dennis

THE MARKET FOR INVESTMENT MANAGEMENT SERVICES

This chapter focuses on the providers of investment management services: the intermediaries who actually get the money into the markets. We distinguish between publicly traded and privately traded assets, because the markets operate in very different ways.

Starting with publicly traded securities, we show how different degrees of market efficiency lead naturally to differences in the ways that service providers behave. Observing their behavior in any market, one can then draw conclusions about the degree of efficiency they perceive to be at work. The text then focuses specifically on indexing, a natural consideration in efficient markets.

For privately traded assets, the private equity market provides an illustration. That presentation completes our three primers for fiduciaries.

THE INVESTMENT MANAGEMENT INDUSTRY

Over the past few years, a discussion has taken place in the United States about the future of the investment management industry. What type of firm will succeed? Will there eventually be a few giant multiproduct firms or will the number of smaller, specialized firms multiply? Richard Ennis raises the discussion to a new level of rigor by invoking arguments from biology and economics.[1] Though his evidence focuses on the U.S. market, his arguments are general and can be applied to any country.

Species adapt to their environments, or they become extinct. In a challenging environment, where risks are great and survival is due mainly to chance, the preferred strategy is to bear large numbers of offspring, with little or no parental investment, hoping that some will survive. When the environment favors a particular species, the preferred strategy is for relatively few offspring, with parental involvement in protecting and nurturing the offspring.

So too with investment management products. The more efficient a market, the more success is a matter of chance. In such an environment, it is reasonable for active managers to focus on product development, launching a proliferation of products. In an inefficient market, managers able to exploit the inefficiencies successfully should invest their resources in nurturing a few products.

Our comment is that there's a lesson here for fiduciaries. Observe the marketplace, and judge for yourself what strategy a particular manager appears to adopt.

That's the biological angle. Now for economics.

Consider passive management first. This portion of the marketplace resembles pure oligopoly. The product is undifferentiated. Economies of scale are significant. Concentrated market shares are the most likely ultimate result, with relatively few suppliers.

Now consider active management:

- In an inefficient market, market share should gravitate to those managers who can most successfully use information and insights. Also, such firms would have no reason to settle for less than a premium price.

- As markets move toward efficiency, consider a market that is marginally inefficient: Some managers can profitably exploit inefficiencies some of the time. As such a manager's portfolio grows, the cost of trading will eventually overcome the informational advantage. In such a market, small managers have an edge, other things being equal.

- In an operationally efficient market (which still allows for some informational inefficiency), monopolistic competition holds. That is, there are many buyers and sellers, products are slightly differentiated (by proprietary technique of security selection), and entry and exit are easy. Here market share should not be concentrated. It should also be unstable, as chance and marketing acumen are important (though not the only) drivers of market share.

By observing the relative proportions of actively and passively managed funds, and the numbers and market shares of various types of product, Ennis shows how to draw conclusions about the degree of market efficiency that exists.

One facet of his observations about U.S. markets is particularly interesting. He notes that active management fees paid by large funds have been static, even though indexing has grown and manager performance has been lackluster. He attributes this to the fact that fiduciaries are buying, not superior performance itself, but the prospect of superior performance. Presumably, this prospect remains as bright as ever in the minds of fiduciaries.

A recent experiment shows that managing fiduciaries see through at least a portion of the hype with which investment managers surround their products. Their own expectations for the degree of outperformance of benchmarks that managers can deliver are distinctly lower than managers claim to be able to deliver. Alas, their actual experience, in the aggregate, is worse than their expectations.[2]

INVESTMENT MANAGEMENT IN TRADED SECURITIES

In countries with developed markets, this is big business: Research, execution, portfolio management, several forms of intermediation, custody, counseling—the list of areas of specialization is long. The amount of money involved is huge. Even where markets are not fully developed, the specialists are there in force.

Active management in traded securities is well understood by fiduciaries. Our focus is therefore on the alternative, passive management, since it is less widely practiced than experience suggests would be wise.

INDEXING

An index is a proxy for investing in an asset class. That means it should reflect the set of investible opportunities in that asset class. In the largest capital markets, the number of available securities is so large that subsets are formed into indexes. These subsets are so formed as to reflect particular characteristics that the index is meant to mimic. For example, they might reflect the whole equity or bond market in a country or around the world, or predefined portions of them.

A comprehensive index in any asset class will be the sum of all the traded securities, if one is willing to exclude those portions of the opportunity set that are closely held and not traded. Thus the index automatically represents the total of all active management. If you invest in the index, you are buying the ideas of all the active participants in that asset class. Strictly, you are not buying their ideas, because you cannot see their ideas. You are buying the implementation of their ideas. However, in publicly (but not privately) traded markets, it is possible to buy the aggregate mechanically, without paying for the research that each active manager conducts. The fee for buying an index fund is therefore much lower than the fee for active management. This gives an indexed portfolio a head start in RANVA (risk-adjusted net value added) calculations. It will also greatly simplify the managing and operating fiduciaries' functions.

Indexing means tracking the actions of not just the best but all the mediocre and poor participants in the market. At first sight, that is not an attractive strategy. You need to have either of two motivations for doing this. First, you must believe that it is not possible to identify the best managers, or that their degree of superiority is less than the fee you would have to pay to hire them. Or second, you must be willing to give up the chance of superior performance in exchange for avoiding the risk of inferior performance.

Many fiduciaries find one or other of these two motivations attractive. Others do not. Some fiduciaries find them attractive in some asset classes but not in others. At the individual level, it is a question of beliefs and preferences, not of right or wrong. But at the aggregate level, when all investors are considered, active investors together perform worse than passive investors do, after investment management fees are taken into account. The justification for active management becomes, "Superior managers exist, and my team has a better chance of identifying them than the average group of fiduciaries and investors." It appears that more people believe this than succeed in profiting from it. Or they are willing to take the risk of being wrong, knowing that more than half of them will be wrong.

In the United States, roughly 18 percent of tax-exempt domestic equity assets represent indexed investing. Foreign equities are roughly 25 percent indexed. Domestic bonds are roughly 6 percent indexed, and foreign bonds 1 percent.[3]

Indexing is usually called passive management. It is not passive in the sense of being action-free. Even a full replication of every security in an index requires action to be taken. Dividends and income have to be collected and reinvested in the right proportions, purchases and sales made as the components of the index change, and so on. And full replication is an unusual way of running an index fund. Frequently, methods that involve sampling are used, the idea being to match the characteristics of the index without the inconvenience and expense of holding all the small securities in it. These methods, which sometimes also include optimization of the holdings, may require more trading than full replication, and typically result in higher tracking error. Or index funds can be created synthetically by combining cash and index futures, and turning over the futures contracts as they mature. This can mean tracking error when the securities and futures markets are mispriced relative to each other.[4]

Indexing is passive to the extent that it can be performed mechanically, once the index rules are prescribed. But quantitative forms of active management can also be performed mechanically, once the approach is specified. What really makes indexing different from active management is that no set of forward predictions, aimed at beating the market, underlies the selection of the securities. But, by definition, indexing is really a combination of all forms of active management. Because of this, it needs to be evaluated as one selection from an opportunity set of all forms of active management. And its selection needs to be monitored as staying appropriate over time.

In particular, two features of indexing need to be monitored.

The first is whether the index truly matches what active managers are doing. The most familiar example of a mismatch is the Morgan Stanley Capital International EAFE (Europe, Australia, and the Far East) equity index. The mismatch arises for two reasons. The index includes a number of securities that foreigners are not allowed to invest in. It therefore is an inaccurate representation of the opportunity set. Also, most managers with a mandate to invest globally consciously choose to underinvest in Japan. They therefore do not make the most of the opportunity set. When an index and active managers are persistently as far apart as in this case, fiduciaries must decide which of the two, or what combination of the two, they take to represent their asset class exposure. Moreover, it is important for governing fiduciaries and their managing fiduciaries to agree on this question.

The same holds true to an even greater extent in moving to less liquid markets, such as emerging markets and real estate. At some stage, the reality is that indexing is just another approach to the asset class, not the average of all active approaches. It may still be an attractive approach, for example, because of cost considerations. But it will not replicate the middle of the range of returns of active managers.

The second feature of indexing that needs to be monitored is the extent to which it may cause a market to become noticeably inefficient. The greater the amount of indexing, the less the amount of active research done in the market. What degree of indexing makes a formerly efficient market inefficient? At 1 percent indexing, there would be virtually no impact at all. At 99 percent indexing, there would be so little research done that the opportunity for making superior decisions with good research is irresistibly tempting. Those are black-and-white conclusions. Nobody knows where the gray area lies.

Two things are known, however.

One is that evidence of inefficiency caused purely by indexing already exists in the U.S. equity market. Between 1977 and 1991, membership in the S&P 500 Index has been worth, on average, more than an additional 2 percent per annum to the shares of member companies.[5] Similarly, in 1990 and 1991, being added to the Russell 2000 (Small Cap) Index was worth more than 2 percent on average to the new member's share price, while being deleted from that index cost more than 2 percent on average.[6] These effects are potentially exploitable by active managers.

The second thing known is that active managers, on the whole, do not realize that potential.

ALTERNATIVE ASSETS

So far, we have focused on publicly traded securities. They are the dominant form of investment for pension funds. The private equity market is an illustration of markets in which information is difficult to acquire. Indeed, the information symmetry between buyers and sellers of services, so heavily assumed and relied on by fiduciaries in their traditional investment media, breaks down spectacularly in the private equity market.

By the private equity market, we mean professionally managed equity investments in the unregistered securities of private and public companies.[7] Private equity is often included in the category "alternative assets." Other assets in this category might be distressed debt, emerging market stocks, real estate, oil and gas, commodities, economically targeted investments, and derivative-based approaches such as managed futures and market-neutral portfolios. We restrict our discussion to private equities in the United States.

THE PRIVATE EQUITY MARKET

The private equity market has three major kinds of players: issuers, intermediaries, and investors. One other kind of player also turns out to be important to pension funds. We call them "information producers."

Issuers tend to share a common trait. Since private equity is one of the most expensive forms of finance, issuers generally are firms that cannot raise financing in the debt market or the public equity market. Issuers of traditional venture capital are young firms, that are most often developing innovative technologies and are projected to show very high growth rates in the future. Since the mid-1980s, however, nonventure private equity investment has outpaced venture investment. For example, middle market companies might use the private equity market to finance changes in capital structure and in ownership. This can be particularly useful when owners of private businesses reach retirement age. Sometimes, public companies that go private issue a combination of debt and private equity to finance their management or leveraged buyout.

Intermediaries—mainly limited partnerships—manage an estimated 80 percent of private equity investments. Under the partnership arrangement, institutional investors are the limited partners and professional private equity managers, working as a team, serve as the general partners. The private equity managers acquire large ownership stakes for themselves and their partners, and take an active role in monitoring and advising portfolio companies. In many cases, they exercise as much control as company insiders, or more.

Public and corporate pension funds are the largest investor groups, together holding roughly 40 percent of capital outstanding. They are followed by endowments and foundations, bank holding companies, and wealthy families and individuals, each of which holds about 10 percent of total private equity. Most institutional investors invest in private equity because they expect the risk-and-cost-adjusted returns on private equity to be higher than the corresponding returns on traditional investments. Other benefits may be total fund diversification, and the smoothness of reported returns resulting from the appraisal process often used for valuing illiquid investments.

Also important in the private equity market is a group of "information producers" whose role has increased greatly in recent years. These are the agents, advisers, and gatekeepers who place private equity, raise funds for private equity partnerships, and evaluate partnerships for potential investors. They exist because they reduce costs associated with the information problems that arise in private equity investing. Agents facilitate the search by private companies for equity capital and the search by limited partnerships for investors. They also advise on the structure, timing, and pricing of private equity issues, and assist in negotiations. Advisers help prospective institutional investors to evaluate limited partnerships. Their value to pension funds arises because most funds are unfamiliar with the workings of the private equity market.

Survival

Recall Ennis's biological analogy. In the challenging environment of private equities, the strategy for success, indeed for survival, is to protect and nurture a few offspring. Observe how the different species act, and understand the requirements for living in this environment.

In 1995, 205 firms were sponsoring limited partnerships. (Contrast this with the thousands of money managers in the world of publicly traded investments.) Of these, the 20 largest are responsible for almost half of the capital involved.[8] Expansion tends to be accommodated not by more firms being created, but by more dollars being invested with the existing firms. Though there are generalists, these firms tend to invest in specialized ways, reflecting the areas they know best. They have experience, expertise, and connections. In what is essentially a deal-driven business, these are colossal advantages. They are also the factors that limit the number of serious players.

The dealmakers generally don't understand the institutional marketplace well. That's why they, too, require intermediaries: the so-called gatekeepers, or advisers, who know the potential institutional investors and do the due diligence research on the deals offered by the general partners. Some pension funds and other investors have developed their own reputations as serious investors in private equities and work directly with the general partners rather than through gatekeepers.

There are about 30 dominant gatekeepers in the U.S. private equity market, and perhaps half are used by pension funds. Gatekeepers tend to come initially from private equity firms or from institutions that invest with them. They cast their nets over many types of general partner specialists, but tend to start with the area of expertise they themselves came from.

All this powerfully confirms that the survival strategy is to protect and nurture a few offspring, rather than to create a proliferation of products and hope that a few survive.

Fees and Returns

The information flow itself has great value. So does the time and expertise required for the difficult due diligence research to identify the best deals and the best dealmakers. Then there is the need to monitor and participate in the issuing businesses. Finally, an exit strategy must be carried out: take the issuing business public or sell it privately. Together these call for higher fees than the active management of securities portfolios. A typical arrangement (though they vary a lot) is for general partners to charge an annual management fee of 1 percent to 2 percent a year. In addition, they take a "carried interest" of around 20 percent of the return on the investments; that is, they split the return 80/20 with the limited partners. Sometimes the carried interest is calculated after a priority return, perhaps the yield on 10-year Treasuries, is first paid to the limited partners.

Gatekeepers charge fees too, but as pension funds, endowments, and foundations learn to acquire the relevant expertise themselves, those fees have fallen. They are now often below 50 basis points a year.

The institutional investors hope to capture a return, net of all fees and carried interests, of either an absolute amount (e.g., 15%–18% a year), or a relative amount (e.g., 3%–5% a year more than publicly traded equities provide). For this to happen, the underlying investments have to earn gross returns of 20 to 25 percent a year, on average.

Individual investments result in hugely different returns. Some are total failures, with the loss of virtually all capital invested. Others have miraculous returns: Everyone is searching for the next Microsoft. The lesson is to diversify one's holdings, not only of individual exposures but also of partnerships invested in.

What have actual returns been? Widely different, and cyclical.

The calculations themselves are not easy. Until a partnership is wound up, no return calculation is definitive. Intermediate calculations require appraisals of the value of nontraded ongoing businesses. These are unreliable. In addition, cash flows occur all the time, not just once at the start and once at the end of the partnership. The amount a pension fund commits to a 10-year partnership is drawn down gradually, perhaps over 5 years, as the businesses require cash. Before the partnership is dissolved, some businesses generate cash, usually from their sale, and the pension fund's share is returned to it. To take the timing of cash flows into account, internal rates of return (IRR) are the measures used to calculate returns on a partnership.

Returns have tended to be cyclical. Investors in partnerships formed in the late 1970s have, in general, received extremely high returns, much higher than the expectations stated earlier. Early word of these successes caused a glut of investors through most of the 1980s, and returns for partnerships formed in those years were generally below the (historically high) publicly traded equity returns. It is too early to judge returns of more recently formed partnerships. But this notion of comparing returns with other partnerships formed in the same "vintage year" is accepted custom.

Another feature of partnership returns is that they are highly dispersed. Even within the same vintage year, the 10-year IRRs vary enormously. Between the upper and lower quartile breaks, differences of 15 percent per annum are common. These are not just differences in a 1-year return: they are differences in 10-year average returns. A comparison of these with the 1-year-return dispersion figures in Table 5.1 shows how wide the dispersion is in private equity markets. No wonder investors feel both that there are huge opportunities for superior management ability in the general partner to reward the investors and that these investments are much more risky than publicly traded equities. Whether the high fees being charged are justified is a matter of ongoing debate, and ongoing negotiation.[9]

NOTES

1. "The Structure of the Investment Management Industry: Revisiting the 'New Paradigm'" by Richard M. Ennis, *Financial Analysts Journal,* July–August 1997. We are grateful to Mr. Ennis for giving us access to his paper before its publication.

2. At an interactive session with clients from around the world in April 1997, Gloria Reeg and Monica Butler of Frank Russell Company asked clients to punch into a machine their expectations for excess returns in each of several asset classes. They then showed the clients what their own investment managers forecast, and what their actual results had been. The subsequent discussion confirmed the observations to which this note refers.

3. These statistics are based on a comprehensive survey reported in the May 12, 1997, issue of *Pensions & Investments.* Including assets subject to "enhanced indexing" (i.e., a systematic active approach overlaid on a basically indexed portfolio) increases the indexed proportion of domestic equities to 21 percent, and of domestic bonds to 9 percent. Including bonds that are immunized or dedicated (i.e., matching a liability rather than an asset benchmark) further increases the indexed proportion of domestic bonds to 12 percent.

4. See "Index Funds" by Stephen Lofthouse, in *Readings in Investment,* edited by Stephen Lofthouse (Chichester, England: John Wiley & Sons, 1994) for the mechanics of index fund investing.

5. See "Are the Reports of Beta's Death Premature?" by Louis K. C. Chan and Josef Lakonishok, in *Readings in Investment* (op. cit.).

6. See "Membership Effects in the Russell 2000 Index" by Eric J. Weigel and Katie B. Weigel, *Russell Research Commentary,* 1992. This also contains a review of other empirical evidence on membership effects, particularly in the S&P 500 Index.

7. This section and the next one are drawn from "The Economics of the Private Equity Market" by George W. Fenn, Nellie Liang, and Stephen Prowse, published by the Board of Governors of the Federal Reserve System, December 1995.

8. The most useful source of statistics in this field is Venture Economics Investor Services, Boston.

9. See, for example, "Private Equity Dust-Up" by Linda Keslar, *Plan Sponsor,* June 1997. The article cites the findings of a critical study commissioned by nine U.S. public pension funds on the practices and fee structures of private equity managers. The study made a number of recommendations on fee structures, oversight, and coinvestment by the private equity managers.

PART THREE
MANAGING THE PENSION FUND BUSINESS

With the excellence paradigm, the fundamentals of pension law and economics, and the economics of the investment and investment management markets in mind, pension fund fiduciaries are ready to tackle the pension fund management challenge. The first thing to get right is the mission and organization design.

The funding and asset allocation policy decisions are the primary determinants of the financial health of pension systems. However, how these policies are implemented is important, too. Equally important is the reality that "what gets measured, gets managed." Only measurement systems that measure and communicate the right things will do.

Smaller pension funds require special attention. They suffer from serious diseconomies of scale in several ways. This translates into generally poorer performance in relation to larger funds. Indexation and outsourcing the managing fiduciary function are two ways out of the box.

7
Effective Pension Fund Governance

Associate yourself with men of good quality if you esteem your own reputation; for 'tis better to be alone than in bad company.

—*George Washington*

THE EFFECTIVE BOARD

As stated in Chapter 3, there are three kinds of fiduciaries: governing, managing, and operating fiduciaries. Members of the board of trustees are the governors of the fund. They are responsible for the governance and ultimately for the investment results. Unless they also choose to act as managing and operating fiduciaries, they do not conduct all the day-to-day activities themselves. Rather, they enunciate the mission, establish the goals and policies, and design a fiduciary structure with appropriate decision rights. Then they delegate day-to-day responsibilities to managing and operating fiduciaries, and monitor the what and the why of the fund's achievements.

This chapter explains how this is done and what distinguishes competent from incompetent boards.

DEFINE THE FUND'S MISSION

Few pension funds today have adopted mission statements. Nevertheless, we believe they are an essential component of excellence and effectiveness in trustees' actions. In this, we agree with the pension fund executives in our 1994 symposium that lack of mission clarity is an important contributing factor to the excellence shortfall. Notably, mission clarity was a statistically significant performance factor in the 1997 study on organization performance versus organization design, cited in Chapter 2.

It is useful, first, to consider mission statements being used by businesses and governments these days. Some of these statements have real meaning and influence the way the firm works. Others are treated as though they are the flavor of the month, along with other buzzwords such as total quality, vision, core competence, and so on. It is not automatic that a mission statement has an impact, even when the leader is serious about it: Much depends on whether the staff chooses to take it seriously. It is, also, not essential for an organization to have a mission statement. Until recently, corporations never thought about a mission statement, and its absence was not considered inimical to success.

In practice, there is no widespread agreement on the definition of a mission statement. It is evident from looking at even a few examples of corporate mission statements that they are all over the map. Some are simple. Some give evidence of having been constructed by a committee, with everyone's favorite phrase included. Some look like statements of business purpose. Others are built around values. Some contain specific objectives. Others are so general as to be compatible with any state of the universe.

Our advice is to ignore the jargon. Go back to basics. Face the questions that need clear answers:

- *What is the purpose of the fund?* As discussed in Chapter 4, there are two potential purposes. The first is to be the primary source of benefit security to the beneficiaries. The second is to be a source of economic advantage to the sponsor. In other words, whether the sponsor is a corporation, union, government, or other entity, the pension fund is important enough that a high return makes it stand out, relative to other sponsors of the same type.

The first applies to almost every pension fund. The second applies to few. Be clear on the second. It requires unusual risk policies and asset class exposures, organizational capabilities, and patient risk tolerance on the part of the sponsor. Whether the sponsor is a corporation, union, government, or other entity, the pension fund is important enough that a high return creates an economic advantage, relative to other sponsors of the same type.

- *Who is affected by the investment return?* Certainly the plan members and the sponsor. Understand the extent to which each is affected, not just as stated in the plan text, but also in the possible ramifications of high or low returns. Understand what each class of stakeholder expects from the return.

- *How does the board define the creation of investment value?* Broadly, there are asset allocation policy decisions and investment implementation decisions. Each type can involve high or low levels of risk, and high or low levels of cost. Seek either to minimize risk and cost, or to achieve a return that more than compensates for the risks and costs incurred. Be clear on which definition of value is chosen.

Answer those questions and the board will have clarity and alignment, the most important benefits from having a mission statement. If the answers take the board further, and help it to construct what it actually calls a mission statement, so much the better.

Boards may not be able to answer these questions in the abstract. The route to the answers that governing fiduciaries agree on may well be circuitous. For example, groups may be more comfortable discussing asset allocation policy without first defining the creation of investment value. That does not matter, as long as the discussion continues.

Process is important. Often others will propose initial answers to the questions posed here: managing fiduciaries, perhaps, or staff or external consultants. It would be a big mistake for governing fiduciaries simply to accept those answers. They need to be passionately committed to the answers. Without the debate that makes their true feelings come to the surface, the odds are they will eventually reveal that they have not adopted the answers as their own. Certainly others can act as consultants in the process, and managing fiduciaries should be heavily involved in applying the logic of the answers; but ideally they should be no more than facilitators of the discussion. Answers that have survived debate about alternatives are much more likely to be accepted as important guides to action. They will also form a valuable and convincing source of education to new fiduciaries and staff members.

Keep the answers short, understandable, and easily remembered: Those are far more valuable characteristics, in practice, than a lumbering, unwieldy statement. A mission statement does not stand alone, and therefore it need not attempt to be all encompassing. There is no prize for putting everything into one run-on sentence.

Perhaps we can be permitted a fanciful digression, to look at mission statements from a totally different perspective. One does not usually think of nations as having mission statements. However, "life, liberty, and the pursuit of happiness" can be thought of as the American mission statement, just as *liberté, égalité, fraternité* ("liberty, equality, brotherhood") represents France. Both these pithy phrases summed up a revolutionary spirit. Perhaps the ferment of change is the time when a mission statement has its best chance of being inspirational. In less troubled times, Canada's "peace, order, and good government" is more typical: less high-sounding, but desirable nevertheless, and definitely reflective of the values Canadians are usually thought to espouse. But is a national mission statement essential to success? Not if one thinks of Great Britain, for which the absence of a written constitution proved no handicap to making a small nation the world's most powerful for a long time.

ESTABLISH GOALS AND POLICIES

We devote three chapters to goals and policies. Chapter 8 deals with funding policy, Chapter 9 with asset allocation policy, and Chapter 10 with implementation policy. Here we simply summarize the issues and considerations involved.

Governing fiduciaries rarely have the right to establish funding policy. But discussions on funding policy are essential to understanding the sponsor's risk tolerance and expectations of the fund's long-term return.

Investment policies, encompassing both asset allocation and implementation, are the single most important focus of governing fiduciaries. The policies adopted will depend on the goals adopted. These in turn will depend on what is best for the stakeholders.

If governing, managing, and operating fiduciaries all do their jobs right, the fund's assets achieve two things that stakeholders value. First, sufficient assets ensure that benefits promised will become benefits paid. Second, the assets produce investment returns that reduce the contribution rate required to support a given stream of benefit payments. The higher the return produced, the lower the contribution rate required. Thus we might call "Deliverable 1" benefit security, and "Deliverable 2" a high fund return. A good board confronts the trade-off between these two deliverables head-on, and fashions investment policies that best balance the financial interests of the stakeholders.

Structuring the fund involves a further important consideration. The pricing of securities in modern financial markets is a highly competitive activity. As a result, rewards are generally in line with the nondiversifiable risks undertaken. Most asset allocation policies could be implemented very cost-effectively through index fund, thus avoiding unnecessary diversifiable risks. Alternatively, governing fiduciaries can choose to join the fray. They can choose to have some or all of the fund's domestic or foreign stocks and bonds actively managed. They can choose to engage in direct investment activities such as real estate or private equity transactions. Or they can choose to engage in some combination of these activities.

All these choices involve delicate judgments. In the end, only the incremental costs and risks of active management are certain. The rewards are not. That is why the architecture of the reward system is so important. Rewards should provide decision makers with incentives that are carefully aligned with the economic interests of the ultimate pension fund stakeholders.

ESTABLISH THE FIDUCIARY STRUCTURE AND DECISION RIGHTS

So far, we have discussed policy issues. These are inescapably in the court of the governing fiduciaries. Executing day-to-day investment decisions and hiring the people who make them are not. Day-to-day decisions require a level of investment expertise that is not an essential qualification for a governor's role. Like a board of directors, governors need to be comfortable making "big picture" decisions. Day-to-day decisions require people who are devoted, every day, to making those decisions. Governors typically are involved in pension fund affairs on a regular but not continuous basis—again, just like a board of directors. True, some governors have the expertise and the time required to be managing or operating fiduciaries. In that case, it is preferable to think of them as wearing two or more hats. The rest of this section deals with issues concerning the separation of fiduciary decisions, on the assumption that different people will be involved.

Operating Fiduciaries

Day-to-day decisions are best made by investment professionals. The types of professional needed are determined by how the governors have defined the creation of investment value, and which asset classes are chosen for fund exposure. The people or organizations hired to fill these roles are the operating fiduciaries. They may be internal employees of the fund or the sponsor, or the work may be outsourced to external professionals or firms. They are fiduciaries because they are given the right to make and execute decisions, albeit within the scope of their mandates. Their roles encompass investment decision making, execution, and custody of assets.

Defining their roles is important. The definition should align responsibility with accountability and the required skills. It should reflect the compensation policy that the governors have adopted. These elements of process are essential for the prudent and profitable delegation of fiduciary responsibilities.

Managing Fiduciaries

Hiring the operating fiduciaries and monitoring that they remain appropriate for their roles, typically require more expertise and time than governing fiduciaries can make available. That is why managing fiduciaries are needed (though, as before, some governing fiduciaries can wear the managing fiduciary's hat).

What is the bundle of expertise that the managing fiduciaries need? They must understand:

- Economic history, especially how financial markets and various forms of financial intermediation have evolved through innovation.

- What makes financial markets efficient—and supportable views on the efficiency of relevant markets.

- Portfolio management processes within the various asset classes, and the assumptions that drive them.

- Principal-agent theory, and how it affects organization architecture, the design of information systems, and a human resources plan for staffing the pension fund organization.

- The key external suppliers of services to the fund.

- Corporate and/or public sector finance, especially as it relates to financial assets and liabilities, the legal and regulatory framework governing pension finance and investments, and practical business management experience.

With these attributes, managing fiduciaries select, hire, and contract with the operating fiduciaries. These aspects are described in Chapter 10. They also monitor the activities of the operating fiduciaries, to ensure that retaining them is still appropriate for the fund. If necessary, they dismiss or replace operating fiduciaries who contravene or fail to fulfill their mandates, or who are no longer required because of a change in the fund's structure. And they prepare reports for the governing fiduciaries, who may delegate responsibilities but can never give up the final, highest level of fiduciary responsibility.

Managing fiduciaries are typically internal employees. Some may be involved part-time in other roles for the fund or the sponsor. Sometimes the role of managing fiduciary is outsourced. Investment consulting firms, in particular, are making themselves available for this role.

There is no uniformity of practice in the compensation of managing fiduciaries. Many persons in this role are compensated as internal salaried employees. Others have incentive arrangements commensurate with the importance of the decisions they make that affect the fund's return. Outsourcing, whether of the managing fiduciary's role or of the operating fiduciary's role, invariably requires incentive compensation. Today, this is usually based on the size of the assets for which responsibility is outsourced. In Chapter 5, in discussing the optimal size of assets under management, and in Chapter 11, when we show how to calculate the risk-adjusted net value added, we suggest other approaches to aligning compensation with stakeholders' interests.

Defining the roles of managing fiduciaries is essential. The definition, like that of operating fiduciaries, should align responsibility with accountability and the required skills. It should reflect the compensation policy that the governors have adopted. These elements of process are crucial for the prudent and profitable delegation of fiduciary responsibilities.

The Fund's CEO

As with any other business, this business deserves a chief executive officer. How the duties are shared between the governing board, the fund's CEO, and the managing fiduciaries will depend on the culture of the country, the culture of the fund sponsor, and the personalities and experience of the governors and the CEO.

It is not typical practice to use the CEO title in making such an appointment. The common view is that only megafunds can afford a CEO to manage the pension fund business. We have a different view: If an organization can afford to sponsor a defined benefit pension plan, it cannot afford not to have a CEO. Remember the median 66 basis points estimated annual excellence shortfall? That means leaving $6.6 million each year on the table for every $1 billion of pension assets. While not enough by itself, hiring or appointing a visible, accountable CEO may well be the most important step a board of governors can take toward taking those 66 basis points off the table and putting them to work in the fund.

There are two reasons this is so. First, by delegating the management of the pension fund to a knowledgeable professional, the board removes the temptation to do the management job itself. There is no surer path to leaving pension fund money on the table than running the fund by inexperienced committee. The second reason relates to the need to align economic interests. The critical operational decisions for the fund must be made by an agent who is accountable to the board, and whose compensation is tied to the success of the pension fund.

In a small fund, the CEO may be the only managing fiduciary. In a large fund, the other managing fiduciaries will report to the CEO. In both cases, the CEO is the link between the managing and governing fiduciaries. The CEO may also be a governing fiduciary. If so, the CEO's role is different from that of the other governing fiduciaries because the CEO takes on the day-to-day management role.

ADDITIONAL SUCCESS FACTORS: TRUST AND CHARACTER

An important additional ingredient for success in creating value is a high level of organizational trust. The governing board will be largely composed of generalists, not investment specialists. The board must be able and willing to look to their team of managing fiduciaries for the advice that will help shape the critical policy decisions. The board must trust the management team sufficiently to delegate the implementation of policy decisions to it, without feeling the need to interfere or second-guess the team's actions.

Frankly, this also makes the board's job less fun. Implementation is where concepts become reality, where abstractions require real people to make things happen. This is where contact with the markets takes place, through fascinating people. It is easy to forget that what governing fiduciaries need from implementation of their policy is not entertainment, but investment value. They need either implementation at the lowest possible cost, or an added return that more than compensates for the added risk and the added cost of active management.

The most common reason many pension funds continue to be "organizationally challenged" is that their governing boards either don't know what their job is, or if they do, are not doing it well. The reverse is also true. Behind every well-run pension fund stands a governing board that knows its job and does it well.[1]

What is the difference between competent and incompetent boards? Competent boards have a preponderance of people of character who are comfortable doing their organizational thinking in multiyear time frames. These people understand ambiguity and uncertainty, and are still prepared to go ahead and make the required judgments and decisions. They know what they don't know. They are prepared to hire a competent CEO and delegate management and operational authority, and are prepared to support a compensation philosophy that ties reward to results.

Boards that lack competence fail to do these things. Sometimes they don't treat all pension plan stakeholders evenhandedly, or don't even fully understand what the pension deal is. They react rather than lead. They crave certainty, and gravitate to those who promise it. They postpone making the key policy decisions indefinitely. They second-guess management and operational decisions. They take credit when things go well, and assign blame elsewhere when they don't. They evaluate results using the wrong benchmarks, and support compensation arrangements that do not align economic interests. Perhaps most damning of all, they do not take the time to find out what they don't know, but should know, to be effective fiduciaries.

Stakeholders do not want to end up with this kind of board. What can be done to assemble and support a competent board of pension fund fiduciaries able and willing to serve? Here is a five-point checklist:

1. *Draw up a governing fiduciary's job description.* This description should focus on the board's responsibility to lead the process for expressing the organization's mission, and to choose the policies most likely to achieve it. It should also focus on the board's role in selecting a CEO and in monitoring organizational effectiveness.

2. *Assemble a group of people who can actually do this job.* This may sound obvious, but pension fund fiduciaries are often chosen for myriad reasons that have nothing to do with their capability. Unfortunately, board selection mechanisms are sometimes so enshrined in tradition or even in law, that they are difficult to change.

3. *Offer the fiduciaries an education program.* Even the most competent board is going to have knowledge gaps that need to be filled. Give them the opportunity to find out what they don't know, but should know, to be effective trustees.[2]

4. *Support the board with consistently high quality staff work.* This raises the level of trust between governing and managing fiduciaries.

5. *Offer board members support in evaluating their own effectiveness.* Nobody is perfect and incapable of improvement, including board members. A good board recognizes this truth.

How important is good governance? The study on organization performance versus organization design, cited in Chapter 2, separated the impacts of good governance, good management, and good operations on pension fund performance. The study found that good governance mattered most.[3]

NOTES

1. The study "Organization Performance versus Organization Design" cited in note 10 in Chapter 2 statistically confirmed the assertion that "behind every well-run pension fund stands a governing board that knows its job, and does it well." The study found that the governance quality scores (i.e., the average scores for the 16 statements in the questionnaire that were governance-related) provided by the 80 pension fund CEOs who participated in the study correlated more highly with organizational performance than either the management quality scores (average of 12 management-related statements) or the operations quality scores (average of 17 operations-related statements). The three correlation coefficients were 0.34, 0.28, and 0.10 respectively. See also Table 2.3 in Chapter 2. Out of the 11 drivers of organization performance listed in the table, 6

statements were governance-related, 4 were management-related, and only 1 was operations-related.

2. The global investment management community now has excellent ongoing educational support through the Association of Investment Management and Research (AIMR), which has over 30,000 members in more than 70 countries. We know of no similar organization dedicated to serving the educational needs of pension fund trustees around the world. Perhaps it is more reasonable to expect the development of national organizations because trustees will want to conform entirely to local legislation.

3. See note 1 above.

8
The Right Funding Policy

Never do today what you can put off till tomorrow.

Punch magazine cartoon, 1849

WHAT IS FUNDING POLICY?

Funding policy means the decisions about the pace at which contributions are made to the pension fund. Defined contribution and multiemployer plans do not permit any flexibility in this regard. Strictly, therefore, funding policy is only relevant for defined benefit and cash balance plans, where either a benefit formula or an investment return is being underwritten by the sponsor.[1]

However, the issues surrounding funding policy are also relevant in certain plans where the contribution rate is fixed. For example, multiemployer plans have fixed contribution rates, but these have to be converted into a benefit level that the fund and future contributions will support. Here, therefore, it is the benefits policy that is flexible, not the funding policy. But the issues linking one fixed policy to one variable policy are sufficiently similar that the discussion in this chapter applies to both.

Typically, investment fiduciaries have no say in funding policy decisions. Their responsibility extends only to the pension fund itself, not to the enforcement of contributions. To that extent, this chapter is a

. But since contributions and investment returns are inti-
ιked in the creation of pension fund wealth, understanding the
sponsoι s funding policy will greatly clarify what is expected from the
investment return. In turn, this will help the fiduciaries construct their
fund mission statement and investment risk policies.[2]

FUNDING POLICY ISSUES

The funding decision for a sponsor consists of three parts:

1. To select a funding target.
2. To select the pace at which the target is attained.
3. To decide whether the current period's contribution should be
   higher or lower than the contribution indicated by the selected
   pace.

To give these ideas a more concrete form, suppose the plan under consideration is a final-three-year-average-pay defined benefit plan that is
currently 90 percent funded using "best estimate" actuarial assumptions. Here is how one corporate sponsor might determine the funding
policy issues:

- I do not want to build any margins into my funding. I will pay for
  the benefits exactly as the plan text defines them. I will take my
  chances that the actuarial assumptions turn out to be accurate; I
  do not want to be cautious and anticipate an unfavorable future.
  Accordingly, I will instruct the actuary to use his best estimates of
  the future in making calculations.

- The 10 percent underfunding has arisen over the years, not caused
  by any single event. I have no problem with the concept of making
  additional payments every year to amortize the unfunded liability.
  There is no obvious time period over which to pay for the shortfall.
  Society has expressed its view in the form of legislation that pre-

scribes the maximum periods over which different kinds of deficit must be made up. I see no reason to make them up faster than legislation requires. I will instruct the actuary to prepare a schedule of payments estimated to make good the entire deficit over the maximum periods permitted. I understand that these payments will decrease over time, and if the actuarial assumptions are realized will cease in 15 years.

- Given the plan's underfunded position, I do not have the option of making no contribution this year. I must pay at least the cost of the coming year's additional accrual of benefits as well as the deficit amortization payment for the year. I see no reason, in the financial position of my corporation, why I should make a higher contribution this year than my decisions on the earlier issues require. I know that a higher contribution is tax-deductible and would reduce the contributions I need to make in future years.

- I would rather keep as much money as possible in my business since that's where I expect to get the best return.

These issues involve only the plan sponsor underwriting the benefits, not the investment fiduciaries. But notice the information available to the fiduciaries.

This sponsor is funding a pension deal that coincides exactly with the written plan text. And the funding is as low as is permissible. There are no hidden margins: no implicit higher benefits, no actuarial margins, no accelerated funding relative to the minimum that the law requires. There is nothing here to cushion any investment risk that is taken. Moreover, since the benefits are currently slightly underfunded, the fund alone does not provide complete benefit security. Beneficiaries depend to some extent on the continuing prosperity of the corporate sponsor for their security. These factors will influence both the mission statement and the investment risk policies of the fund.

Not all situations are similar. Some benefits are overfunded, sometimes massively so. Some corporations build hidden margins into the valuation of their assets and liabilities, using methods explained later in this chapter. These are found most notably in North American plans for union employees, where there is a history of negotiated improvements to benefit levels.

Multiemployer plans are a little bit different. For these plans, the contribution rate is fixed. Also, the investment fiduciaries are typically constituted as the board of governing fiduciaries of the fund. Their responsibilities typically include a decision about the benefit level to be paid until the next valuation. Actuaries help them to estimate the benefit level that the fund and future contributions can support. They frequently build in a contingency margin, to avoid having to reduce benefits if their estimates turn out to be too rosy.

Governments like to use actuarial methods and assumptions that are stable over time. They tend to do this even when times are changing rapidly and it would be reasonable to change their assumptions. Their viewpoint is usually very long term. This means that there are frequently hidden margins—sometimes positive, sometimes negative—in their formal valuation reports. Investment fiduciaries for government funds should take particular care to clarify the margin situation.

In practice, funding and investment issues come together if the investment fiduciaries are also executives in the sponsor's organization. If there is a separation between the two entities, the likely result is a lack of clarity in understanding how each affects the other. One reason is that the investment fiduciaries are unlikely to know much about the adopted funding policy, because funding policy is rarely explicit. The issues tend not to be considered explicitly in the three-stage formulation outlined earlier. Indeed, there is very little literature on the subject.[3] Rather, financial intuition and experience are invoked in making contribution decisions. Our guess is that this has worked well. But it is always worthwhile to go through the issues explicitly. An explicit understanding cannot possibly lead to worse decisions being made; sometimes, though, it will improve the decisions.

THE FUNDING TARGET

The selection of a funding target involves two considerations. First, what benefits have been promised? Second, should we accumulate any reserves in the fund in case the world turns out to be less favorable than our best estimates imply? Answers to these two questions are implemented by the actuary's choice of assumptions and methods in the funding report.[4]

What benefits have been promised? This takes us back to the implicit pension deal discussed in Chapter 4. The benefits may simply be those defined in the plan document; or they may go beyond those benefits, if there is an implicit understanding or a history of periodic improvements.

In principle, several levels of benefits can be considered:

- The benefits accrued to date. These would be based entirely on history, with no projection of salary, service, or plan improvements.
- The benefits accrued to date, including salary projections where relevant, but no future service or plan improvements.
- The benefits likely to be paid ultimately, including salary projections, future service, and possible plan improvements.

Depending on how well funded the benefits are, and on legislation in different countries, one level of benefits may be more relevant than the others when funding decisions are made.[5] In North America, only the promised benefits can be taken into account explicitly. Possible plan improvements cannot be considered. If the sponsor wants to create a reserve in advance for paying a higher level of benefits, the only way is to do it implicitly by overvaluing the current promise. In turn, this overvaluation is achieved by the actuary using a set of assumptions that, in aggregate, are cautious in their view of the future. The degree of caution is rarely made explicit; indeed, it is rarely estimated, because there is no universally held view of what the future will bring. It is a matter of personal judgment, and if sponsor and actuary adopt a cautious view within a range commonly accepted as reasonable, nobody questions that judgment.

What other reserves might the sponsor wish to accumulate in the fund? Typically there have been two.

The first is a reserve against an adverse future. Today's best estimates of the future may turn out to have been optimistic. The cost of the promised benefits will then turn out to be higher than today's best expectation. The sponsor can create a contingency reserve against this possibility by the same implicit device of having the actuary use assumptions about the future that in aggregate contain a margin of caution. In effect, the sponsor deliberately pays somewhat more than the best expectation of the cost.

Another method of building in a margin of caution is to value the fund's assets at less than their market value. The expressions "actuarial value" and "market-related value" are indications that this is happening. Typically, these values are calculated on the premise that there is some central tendency to the investment return. Only the central tendency is credited in the actuarial valuation of the assets. The idea is that fluctuations from the central value are transient, will correct themselves, and are inappropriate in calculating the stream of future contributions. When recent returns have been high, the use of an actuarial value below market value effectively creates a contingency reserve against future lower returns. The reverse is true when recent returns have been low and the actuarial value placed on the assets exceeds their market value. Such a relationship means that the actuary effectively anticipates a higher future return, and has valued the assets as if they have received that higher return. The implicit contingency reserve in the asset value is then negative.

The second reserve that a sponsor may want to accumulate is a reserve against the average age of the active members increasing. This may be particularly relevant when a plan has been closed to new entrants. The older a group of active members, the higher the cost of each year's accrual of benefits. To anticipate and avoid the increase as the group ages, it is possible to estimate each year's contribution in the future for the group, and then estimate the level contribution that would accumulate to the same amount by the time the group retires. The most common actuarial method for performing this calculation is the "entry age" method. In contrast the "unit credit" method looks only at the past and one year's future benefit accrual, so it does not incorporate the aging feature.

The use of the entry age method implies that a reserve is being accumulated, beyond what the unit credit method asks for. While the actuarial underpinnings of the entry age method imply a reserve against an aging of the active members, in fact the reserve can be used for any legitimate purpose. This method is most commonly used in flat benefit plans, where an improvement in the current level of benefits is a reasonable expectation, and in multiemployer plans. The latter are often bargained as defined contribution plans and actuarially transformed into defined benefit plans. They require a margin of caution because it is the fund rather than the employers that must underwrite the benefits.[6] Benefits are reduced if the fund is not large enough to support them.

THE PACE AT WHICH THE TARGET IS ATTAINED

It should be clear by now that the actuarial values placed on the plan's promised benefits have a purpose that can go beyond a best estimate of their value. That is why we have used the expression *funding target,* which better describes the concept. But "funding target" will not be found in a formal actuarial report. Instead the word "liabilities" is used. Similarly, the word "assets" is used, regardless of the value placed by the actuary on the fund's holdings.

If the assets exceed the liabilities, the funding target has already been attained. If the liabilities exceed the assets, the sponsor has a choice of deciding how fast to catch up. Legislation exists to specify the maximum contribution and the minimum contribution that can be made each year.[7] The sponsor's decision is essentially twofold. First, at what normal pace should we catch up? Second, should we make this year an exceptional year? This section presents the considerations relevant to the normal pace.

Essentially, there are three sets of considerations:

1. Will we earn a higher return in our enterprise or in the pension fund?
2. Is there evenhanded treatment of surplus and deficit?
3. How will interested parties view the relationship between assets and liabilities?

Will We Earn a Higher Return in Our Enterprise or in the Pension Fund?

The first consideration is the alternative use of the contribution. The pension fund return accrues tax-free in many countries, with Australia a notable exception. Corporate earnings are taxed, but for many corporations their financial position may enable the impact of the tax to be deferred. Governments have social returns, rather than purely financial returns, to consider. In all cases, enterprises will have their own ideas as to what returns are reasonable on their own ventures and in the capital markets generally. This issue, therefore, can be resolved using typical capital budgeting techniques.

Is There Evenhanded Treatment of Surplus and Deficit?

The second consideration is the evenhanded treatment of surplus and deficit. The many issues here can perhaps best be illustrated by focusing on the American scene, where the treatment is far from evenhanded.

Corporate contributions are tax-deductible when made and are taxed when withdrawn from the fund. But the tax rates are not identical. Rather, in addition to the normal corporate tax rate, there is an additional excise tax of 50 percent of the amount of surplus withdrawn and reverting to the employer. And surplus can only be withdrawn when a plan is terminated. This 50 percent rate drops to 20 percent, provided either that an amount equal to at least 20 percent of the reversion is first used to make pro rata improvements to accrued benefits, or at least 25 percent of the terminated plan's surplus is first transferred to a replacement plan.

In practice, then, these penal conditions mean that surplus cannot be used rapidly. It can only be drawn down gradually to pay for one year's worth of benefit accrual at a time. And if the investment return on the surplus exceeds one year's benefit accrual, then the surplus itself keeps growing. This has been the case with many pension funds through the long period of historically high returns that markets have provided since the early 1980s.

This lack of symmetry in the treatment of surplus and deficit is an extremely powerful factor in impelling corporate sponsors, particularly publicly traded ones, to avoid building up surplus. While it takes a dollar out of the corporation to put a dollar into the pension fund, the share price will not reflect the full value of that dollar once it shows up as a dollar of pension surplus.

How Will Interested Parties View the Relationship between Assets and Liabilities?

How interested parties view the fund's surplus or deficit position is still evolving.

Today, most large employers and unions understand the meaning of pension issues very well, and know how to go behind the reported figures to make their own assessments of what is important to them. As they track a situation, they find few surprises. Equally, leading financial analysts have come to understand the subtleties of pension accounting. They view the new disclosures as shedding light on previously hidden areas, rather than as fundamentally changing things. Only in extreme situations do the new disclosures actually influence action.

One of the extreme situations is particularly interesting. Corporations with large pension surpluses become more attractive as takeover targets, because the surplus can be used to offset a pension deficiency in another corporation. This effectively enables the surplus to be used instantly rather than gradually.

We have seen one other noteworthy, and perhaps surprising, response to the perceptions of others.

Working with large pension funds, we come across many situations where they are underfunded. Inevitably, the dollar size of the deficit tends to be large, even when the ratio of assets to liabilities is close to 100 percent. In the United States, this places funds with large unfunded liabilities on the list of the 50 worst funded pension plans published annually by the Pension Benefit Guaranty Corporation (PBGC). Since the PBGC insures dollar amounts, a classification by unfunded dollars is appropriate for them, even though benefit security provided by a pension fund is better measured in percentage terms as far as a beneficiary is concerned. Many corporations become very upset if they appear on this list and removing themselves from it sometimes becomes a factor in their funding and investment policies.

SHOULD THIS BE AN EXCEPTIONAL YEAR?

Decisions on the two previous issues (what is the funding target, and at what pace should we attain it) constitute the funding policy. Whether to make the current period's contribution in line with policy or to deviate temporarily from policy is the final funding question. We observe simply that the sponsor's ability to direct the required cash flow, and the tax implications, dominate this decision. Sponsors should be, and usually are, thoroughly familiar with these issues.

NOTES

1. Cash balance plans are discussed extensively in Chapter 15. Multiemployer plans are found in unionized industries, where the union, sometimes with an association of employers, sponsors a pension plan. Under a collective bargaining agreement, employers agree to contribute a certain amount to the fund for each hour worked by a union employee. The fund's trustees are responsible for converting the contributions into a benefit formula that can be supported by contributions and future investment returns.

2. When searching for articles to explain the actuarial process, the U.S.-based Financial Accounting Standards Board identified two in its classic 1981 Discussion Memorandum on Employers' Reporting for Pensions and Other Post-Employment Benefits. These were "Unfunded Pension Liabilities . . . the New Myth" by Paul A. Gewirtz and Robert C. Phillips, initially published in *Financial Executive,* August 1978, and "How Actuaries Determine the Unfunded Pension Liability" by D. Don Ezra, originally published in *Financial Analysts Journal,* July/August 1980.

3. Chapter 3 in *Pension Funds and the Bottom Line* by Keith P. Ambachtsheer (Homewood, IL: Dow Jones-Irwin, 1986) is one of few guides to some of the relevant considerations. See also "Asset Allocation and

Funding Policy for Corporate-Sponsored Defined-Benefit Pension Plans" by Michael W. Peskin, *Journal of Portfolio Management,* Winter 1997.

4. Actuaries prepare reports for a bewildering variety of reasons. Perhaps the worst jurisdiction is the United States, which requires liability calculations for regular funding, Retirement Protection Act of 1994 funding, PBGC variable premium, PBGC plan termination, accounting, and perhaps other purposes that we have not caught. Each is performed using a different discount rate, and some statutes specify transition rules for calculating discount rates as they move from one rule to another.

5. This explanation relates to North America. Different considerations apply in other countries. For example, in Japan liabilities have been required to be discounted at 5.5 percent per annum. When long bond yields are much lower, the requirement amounts to a large understatement of the liabilities being valued. In the United Kingdom, recent attention has been focused on the mechanics of meeting the Minimum Funding Requirement (MFR). Benefits that are underfunded by the criteria of this calculation must be made fully funded rapidly. For schemes at or near this position, preservation of a fully funded MFR position appears likely to become an important consideration when investment policy is decided. Another feature of the U.K. scene is the way in which actuaries tend to value equities: not via an explicit or smoothed market value, but by projecting a stream of dividend payments at an assumed growth rate and capturing a present value by using a discount rate. With the recent change in a fund's ability to reclaim Advance Corporation Tax, this may result in more of a write-down in actuarial equity values than the equity market indicates. Or it may prompt a different method of valuing equities.

   In the Netherlands, liabilities are required to be discounted at no higher than 4 percent per annum. Moreover, pension funds must show a return of 4 percent per annum, valuing bonds at amortized cost and equities at market, or potentially face accelerated funding. The focus on solvency has traditionally been regarded as more important than value creation. This might partially explain the cautious approach to asset allocation policy there, and the resulting high cost of DB schemes.

6. This is an oversimplification of the American situation, where employers withdrawing from the plan are responsible for a share of the unfunded liability.

7. Legislation governing contribution limits varies from immensely complicated to relatively simple, with a tendency to ever-increasing complexity throughout the world.

9

The Right Asset
Allocation Policy

As far as the laws of mathematics refer to reality, they are not certain, and as far as they are certain, they do not refer to reality.

—Albert Einstein

INVESTMENT POLICY

Investment policy covers many issues. It starts with beliefs about the future, proceeds to return expectations, and from there to decisions about asset allocation and the asset class arrangements to be adopted. Document not only the decisions and the arrangements, but also the underlying beliefs. That is the path of greatest clarity. It is also very difficult, because it forces a discussion of issues on which reasonable people can validly disagree.

This chapter deals with the most important element of investment policy: asset allocation policy. Other elements of investment policy will be covered in Chapter 10, which focuses on the investment arrangements by which policy is implemented.

This chapter is not about the importance of numbers or the ability to forecast the future accurately. Rather, it is about the thought process that governing fiduciaries need to master. "Prudence is process," we remarked earlier. Here are the process elements.

ASSET ALLOCATION POLICY

The understanding of asset allocation policy has evolved over time and today may be said to have two important characteristics:

1. It assumes an equilibrium investment environment. This means that asset classes are fairly priced relative to each other: The only way to obtain a higher expected return is to take on a larger amount of risk. Exploiting perceived mispricing is recognized as a different issue, known as tactical asset allocation.
2. Mathematical models are extensively used before a governing board sets the policy for its fund.

With this background, decision makers should understand the five elements of the decision process for setting asset allocation policy:

1. What system are we modeling?
2. What are our goals and fears?
3. How shall we model the future?
4. How shall we make a decision?
5. What course should we follow until the next decision?

WHAT SYSTEM ARE WE MODELING?

Mathematical models are used as a rough—not exact—way to capture the workings of a financial system through a series of equations. Invariably, systems are too complex to be modeled as anything other than an approximate representation of what actually occurs.

In pension fund modeling, the system under consideration is the liabilities, the assets, or both assets and liabilities together. The financial position of the sponsor may also be taken into account when liability-related considerations are involved. The days when pension fund assets alone were modeled for a defined benefit plan are long past. The need to consider benefit security makes it essential to consider the liabilities. But the treatment of liabilities is not always on a par with the treatment of assets.

Assets have markets in which they are traded. It is a fact of life that market values change as new information arrives and as the economic environment changes. But pension promises are valued by an actuarial assessment process, periodically rather than continuously. Experience shows that assessed values are typically artificially stable. They are more like book values than market values.

Mixing market values of equities with book values of bonds is not a way to model both asset classes consistently. Neither is the mixture of market values of assets and artificially stable values of liabilities. Essentially, this does not model liabilities. It uses them merely as a device to translate asset returns into measures that involve the liabilities, such as projected funded ratios or contributions or some similar derived measure.

Because there are so many ways to value liabilities for different purposes, what is a sensible approach? There is no alternative but to construct some model of the actuarial decision process itself, or its impact on liability values. This is the equivalent of modeling the market's asset valuation process, or its impact on returns. We have seen many ingenious ways of doing this.

Some move actuarial discount rates in almost perfect correlation with bond yields. Others build stickiness into the changes in the discount rate: no change unless bond yields change by more than some hurdle amount, and even then only a partial movement in the direction of change of bond yields. Others skip the discount rate and proceed directly to the construction of a "liability return." This is the return that would be necessary to keep a fully funded pension plan fully funded, if the liabilities at the start and end of the period were calculated on the basis of discount rates consistent with bond yields. The liability return then becomes a hurdle rate that the fiduciaries hope to exceed with the fund's assets.

There are other issues in modeling the actuarial decision process. For example, how should the gap change between the discount rate and the rate at which wages or salaries are projected to increase? The way in which this innocent question is answered can predetermine which asset classes appear risky and which asset classes appear safe.[1]

Though the sponsor's financial position is not often taken into account explicitly, it is also relevant. The same set of contributions may have different values to different sponsors, because their cost of capital is different. Similarly, the lack of symmetry in treatment of surplus and deficit may cause the same surplus to have unlike values in the eyes of different sponsors. These differences can have significant impacts on the asset allocation policies that appeal to sponsors.[2]

Our purpose here is to warn fiduciaries that they need to understand the characteristics and limitations of the models they use. What are the areas of the pension system that are modeled? What are the main characteristics of the models? How have the sponsor's own financial characteristics been taken into account? Models are of no value unless they provide insights. Insights will not arise in an area that is not modeled, or poorly modeled.

WHAT ARE OUR GOALS AND FEARS?

The governing fiduciaries must consider the interests of the stakeholders.

By definition, the first goal for any pension fund that underwrites defined benefits or investment returns is to secure those benefits or returns. This takes into account the interests of the most important group of stakeholders, the beneficiaries. And it leads to an obvious measure to track. Compare the value of the fund's assets with the value of the promises accrued to date. This is a sine qua non for any governing board.

The second goal is to do so at an acceptable cost to the sponsor. (Once the interests of beneficiaries and sponsors have been considered, the interests of other stakeholders rarely cause a change in goals.) This goal translates loosely into the investment objective of seeking an acceptable level of expected return at an acceptable level of investment risk. What "acceptable" means will vary according to the circumstances of each case. Governing fiduciaries cannot make sensible policy decisions unless they understand what the sponsor wants to achieve and how much of each of many types of risk the sponsor is willing to accept in pursuit of those goals.

Goals and risks share three characteristics: (1) There are many goals and fears; (2) they extend over different periods of time; (3) they are difficult to specify in advance. Each characteristic is important.

There Are Many Goals and Fears

Some relate to the pension system as a whole. Low contributions, or perhaps none at all; low volatility of contributions (sponsors love predictability); low pension expense; low volatility of pension expense; no liability to be shown on the sponsor's own balance sheet; and so on. Often, instead of volatility, the goal is a one-sided measure: no increase in contributions or expense.[3] Similarly for multiemployer plans, goals and fears include a high unit of benefit, no more than a small likelihood that the unit will fall in the future, and so on.

Other goals relate to the investment return only. The most frequent is to beat the median return (often, more in hope than in expectation, the upper quartile break) of a defined group of other funds. Also seen frequently is the desire to beat the actuarial discount rate. This comes from governing fiduciaries who forget the complex history of how the discount rate is chosen.

In many cases, the goals are inconsistent. For example, the more you strive for a high return or low contribution rate, the more volatility you typically have to accept. But specifying inconsistent goals can be constructive. It forces considerations of trade-off, because trade-off there invariably has to be. In practice, no goal ever has its probability maximized and no fear ever has its probability minimized. They are all compromised.

Goals and Fears Extend over Different Time Horizons

Achieving or avoiding some outcome over one year may be important. Other goals or fears may coincide with a sponsor's planning horizon, frequently five years. Others again are very long term, because that is the nature of pension promises.

It is unnatural to think that a single horizon covers all goals and fears. Yet that is often how asset allocation studies are conducted. Usually this is because an optimizer is used in the study, and it is incapable of accepting more than one horizon. The sole use of an optimizer is as an aid to decision making, and invariably the optimizer's solution is rejected in practice. It is unproductive to restrict the formulation of the problem to fit a decision-making tool that will not be used to make the decision. An alternative is to forsake the use of an optimizer and simply perform a large number of simulations.

Goals and Fears Are Difficult to Specify in Advance

For several reasons, a multistage dialogue, involving trial and error, is necessary before decision makers are satisfied.

First, it is difficult to know intuitively what is possible. For example, suppose you are currently underfunded and want the benefits to be fully funded in five years. Is it reasonable to expect the markets to deliver a sufficiently high return to achieve this? Or is it really a question of funding policy: How much is the sponsor prepared to contribute in order to get there? Again, suppose you want to avoid an increase of $1 million in the pension expense over the next five years. Given the normal volatility of markets, is $1 million well within the normal range of uncertainty? Are there actuarial and accounting levers that can be pulled to solve the problem, rather than asset allocation policy? Without initial simulations, it is difficult to know what goals are within the realm of feasibility.

Another reason is that the sponsor's senior management, or the governing fiduciaries, may not actually be involved in the discussion until their staff present a study for consideration. At that stage, senior management or the governing board may be asked to ratify a policy selected by the staff. This may cause new goals and fears, which the staff did not anticipate, to be revealed for the first time. Or the policy may be approved, with only a perfunctory involvement of the decision makers. This is the surest path to regret.

For regret often rears its head later. Regret is rarely discussed in advance of policy setting: It is only experience that makes you conscious of its power. Intellectually, you can consider a bad outcome. You can accept, in advance, some possibility that it will occur. But rarely can you truly feel, in your gut, the same feeling that materializes after the fact if the bad outcome actually happens. Because of this, dealing with the intellectual notion of risk is not enough. The emotional reality of regret should not be ignored. In practice, a governing fiduciary's risk tolerance is frequently lower after the fact than it was specified to be before the fact. This is not easy to take into account. But the first step is to recognize that regret is a human tendency, and the more you can anticipate what will cause regret, the better your chance of avoiding it.[4]

In practice, many goals are not explicitly considered because they are never articulated. They relate to dimensions of comfort that have nothing to do with investment or financial outcomes.[5]

HOW SHALL WE MODEL THE FUTURE?

In modeling the future, you are making a forecast.

Some find it difficult to accept this simple fact. They say, "This is only a model." That is true. What is more, the model usually specifies several possible future outcomes, not just one. That does not make it any less of a forecast. You cannot get around it by saying, "This model simply replicates the past," or the past adjusted by inflation, or the past adjusted by current starting conditions. Whatever you use relates to the future and therefore is a forecast, pure and simple.

There is no obviously right way to make a forecast. Whatever forecast you use, it should have these characteristics:

- *It should be credible.* Users should believe it represents their best effort to model the future. It should be consistent with current market and economic conditions, because that is where the future starts. Sometimes, a forecast gains credibility by comparing it with history. Then, at least, significant similarities and significant differences become apparent and can be discussed.[6]

- *It should reflect your fundamental beliefs.* These might involve the relationships between equity and fixed income returns, between different kinds of equities, between different kinds of fixed income, between liquid and illiquid markets, between asset and liability characteristics, and so on. They might involve a case for history repeating itself or for the future changing in a particular way. Whichever beliefs are incorporated into the forecasts, specify them, along with the reasons for holding them.

• *It should be consistent with the specification of goals and fears.* For example, if goals extend over half a dozen time horizons, the forecast must be relevant to each of those horizons.

HOW SHALL WE MAKE A DECISION?

At this stage, we have built a model of whatever we have chosen to study, we have defined our goals and fears, and we have found a credible way to describe the future. Next, we get some output from all this. Now comes the final test: What asset allocation policy should we adopt? How should we go about making a decision?

This is an exercise in uncertainty, not in mathematical precision. Our model is not the framework of the future; it is an estimate of that framework. The model is itself inaccurate, and there is no way to tell how inaccurate it is. The specified parameters are not the true parameters; they are estimates of the true parameters.

Most decision makers do the appropriate thing. They treat the study as very valuable and informative. They use it to understand the direction in which they must move and this helps them feel more comfortable, or perhaps less uncomfortable. They do not adopt some mathematically precise solution.

Others do not like uncertainty and seek mathematical precision rather than comfort. This is the surest way to be hurt by the future. As an example, consider the technique most often used today in North America: the efficient frontier. This technique purports to define, for every level of fund return volatility, the highest possible expected return and the asset allocation mix that creates it. This is very appealing.

However, the inputs (expected returns for the asset classes, their expected volatility, their covariance structure) are bound to be wrong, once the future unfolds. And it usually turns out that the inputs that are most wrong, in retrospect, are precisely the ones that most influenced the composition of the efficient allocations. In this sense, the technique may indeed be "efficient" when looking forward, but it can be a forecasting error maximizer when looking back.[7] That provides several clues for appropriate use of the asset allocation study. The most experienced governing fiduciaries will tell you to treat the numbers with respect, but not with awe.

Don't Consider Too Many Asset Classes

You will inevitably have some with similar characteristics. If you use an optimizer, it will artificially prescribe some and eliminate others, based on minor differences in specifications. This is error maximization. Give the optimizer a chance to give you useful information, by using only asset classes with widely different characteristics. Think broadly at this stage, and leave smaller differences to the implementation stage.

Don't Confuse Liquid and Illiquid Asset Classes

Liquid asset classes tend to be well researched and traded frequently in efficient markets with low transaction costs. They are priced in line with their covariance with other liquid asset classes. This implies that historical return calculations are reliable and based on many trades. Also, their returns, variances, and covariances offer a rich description of their characteristics. With illiquid asset classes, typically trades are infrequent and historical return calculations are based on few trades or on appraised values. These are not reliable for understanding the asset class and modeling the future. Nor are their prices based on covariance. Their characteristics require specification of illiquidity and possibly many other forms of risk.

If the model does not accommodate their characteristics, so be it. The appropriate allocation to them will then become less a matter of modeling and more a matter of considering characteristics that are not in the model. This makes it all the more important to document the beliefs underlying the exposure.

Most pension funds do not invest in private market assets (with the exception of real estate). In the United States, many large defined benefit funds and most large endowments and foundations do. Illiquid asset classes are not suitable for market timing purposes. They require a long-term commitment, through good times and bad. To make the category of privately traded assets a permanent part of the fund's asset allocation policy requires "yes" answers to these questions:

- Are you willing to take investment risk?
- Do you believe this asset category will produce returns that more than compensate for the costs and risks involved?
- Are you willing to make a material commitment to the category (say, 5%–10% of the fund)?
- Do you have the patience to keep your commitment through bad times (and through times when one does not know whether they're good or bad, because there is no reliable performance measurement for guidance)?
- Do you have the restraint to let your managing fiduciaries act on the fund's behalf? (There are many reasons why governing fiduciaries reserve to themselves the ultimate right to decide on specific deals. One is that deals are intrinsically more interesting than securities. Another is that this is a glamorous arena. Where else is a governing fiduciary likely to experience a partner of the famous firm of Kohlberg, Kravis & Roberts coming to ask for money? Yet another is that deals sometimes blow up, leading—if the fiduciary holds public office—to the embarrassment of adverse front-page publicity.)

These last two questions are easier to handle if you have, in the past, experienced regret in connection with a major decision, and not let that regret affect your next similar decision. (Have you? Be honest!) And remember Keynes's dictum: "Worldly wisdom teaches us that it is better for reputation to fail conventionally than to succeed unconventionally."

If, after all this, you're ready to make a commitment to privately traded assets, you're likely to be a reliable partner in this fascinating world.

Compare the Output Characteristics of a Number of
Asset Allocation Policies

Don't restrict yourself to one that is characterized as optimal. Being close to optimal is enough, since mathematical precision here can be misleading. Also, you rarely know what your true goals and fears are. Early output from the study can identify which ones are difficult to achieve or avoid. Then you can concentrate more closely on modifying those in the next stage of the interactive work process.

Two allocations, in particular, can have conceptual importance.

One is the lowest risk allocation. This is the allocation that comes closest to matching the investment characteristics of the benefit promise, in terms of length, correlation with inflation, and so on. How close does it actually come to matching the promise? Are there feasible allocations that have much higher expected returns with an acceptable level of mismatch? Much of the time, these questions are omitted in a study. The reason is usually that the governing fiduciaries have an intuitive idea of what the lowest risk allocation is, and know in advance that it sacrifices too much potential expected return. Virtually nobody actually adopts the lowest risk allocation. The practical search is for a portfolio that accepts mismatch and strives for a higher expected return.

The second allocation of conceptual importance is the average held by competitors making a similar promise. The reason could be as explicit as being derived from a mission statement that seeks a competitive return. Or it could be as implicit as a desire to avoid maverick risk (the regret that can arise when your unusual policy has performed worse than the traditional policy adopted by your peers).

In practice, most studies consider allocations on either side of the competitive average. That is not a problem. The real problem is deciding what specific allocation is most comfortable to the decision maker. And the reason is that it is difficult to feel differently about the potential impacts of various allocations.

Figure 9.1 illustrates this point. It shows the percentile distribution of the ranges of corporate contributions projected to be made by one particular sponsor in five years' time under the current funding policy. It leaves out the highest 5 percent of each range as well as the lowest 5 percent. Each bar shows the range for an asset allocation policy. The bar on

$ Million

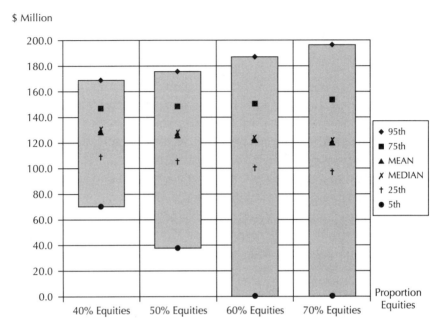

FIGURE 9.1 Ranges of Possible Contributions Five Years Hence with Different Asset Allocation Policies.

the extreme left represents a policy that is most simply characterized as having an equity exposure of 40 percent. Each successive bar to the right changes the policy by adding 10 percent to the equity exposure. Thus the bar to the extreme right represents an equity exposure of 70 percent.

Most decision makers have extreme difficulty in saying that any of these is intrinsically and by far the most comfortable. Every allocation is comfortable if returns turn out to be high and uncomfortable if returns turn out to be low. The allocation with the most favorable expected (mean or median) outcome is also the allocation with the widest possible range. Decision makers tend not to decide by looking at the extremes of the distribution, which have little chance of occurring; they prefer to look at the middle, where the likelihood is higher. But the middle 50 percent of each range (between the 25th and 75th percentiles) is roughly the same size. You can test the impact of high and low returns on other goals and fears. They all tend to share the characteristics shown in Figure 9.1.

That is why maverick risk tends to be so important in practice. If there is no obvious way to tell whether you should be more or less aggressive than your competitors, why not match them? It eliminates maverick risk. Of course, having a different mission statement, or different goals and fears, or benefit promises, or member demographics, or different expectations about capital market prospects—all these will justify being unlike your competitors.

Ultimately, there are only two overriding rules. First, understand the options and their possible impacts. Second, document your reasons for your choice.

WHAT COURSE SHOULD WE FOLLOW UNTIL THE NEXT DECISION?

Nothing stays the same. Right after the asset allocation policy decision is implemented, market movements will change the fund's allocation. In the absence of tactical considerations, should you let the new allocation stand? Should you rebalance to the selected policy? Is there another option?

Many historical studies have been performed, each pointing out that a fund would have gained (or lost) by a certain course of action, such as rebalancing every year. The studies are misdirected. Their conclusions are necessarily time-period-specific. In any case, be wary of advice to adopt a nonthinking, mechanical course of action that is meant to add value. Actually, the matter is much simpler than the multiplicity of studies suggests.

Recall why the particular policy has been chosen. It is the most comfortable. The only reason to rebalance, therefore, is that the new asset allocation is less comfortable. It has nothing to do with the passage of time. Discomfort means we should rebalance, whether discomfort arises after a decade, a year, or a day.

Two factors mitigate the need to rebalance. One is that comfort is not easy to define. As shown earlier, within a surprisingly wide range you might feel unable to distinguish levels of comfort. The second is that rebalancing requires a transaction. It costs money, and like discomfort, that too is negative. The solution is to refrain from rebalancing until the discomfort outweighs its cost.

Economists build mathematical models of comfort, or "utility" as they call it. One study used the most typical of these utility models, linked to a range of levels of risk tolerance and transaction costs. It measured the deviation that ought to be permitted to occur before rebalancing becomes the superior course of action. The range depends on many factors, including the number of asset classes and whether the asset classes deviating most from their policy positions are broadly similar (such as several kinds of equities) or broadly dissimilar (such as equities and fixed income securities).

Three conclusions are of particular interest. The first is that, for a wide range of cases, rebalancing is definitely worthwhile once an asset class is at least 5 percent away from its policy allocation. The second is that rebalancing is most worthwhile across the equity/fixed income allocations, rather than within equities or within fixed income. The third, which is hardly a surprise, is that rebalancing is best done with new cash flow, since that incurs the smallest transaction costs.[8]

It is not difficult to have similar calculations performed to your own specifications. Then decide on, and document, the fund's rebalancing policy.

Is there another option? One that may have promise is in its infancy.

Suppose your goals involve more than one time period. One year from now, you would like to preserve the fund's current 100 percent funded ratio. Five years from now, you would like it to increase to 110 percent. Intuition suggests you might want to adopt a cautious policy in the first year, then a more aggressive one.

Traditional asset allocation models prescribe a single, static policy, rather than a series of allocations that better fit multiple goals and horizons. A relatively new technique called multiperiod stochastic optimization allows for the fact that you will have the opportunity to change the policy. If indeed a static policy is the most sensible, the model will say so. Otherwise it will prescribe a change in policy at a given time, for a given reason. While all our caveats about treating the output with respect rather than awe remain valid, the flexibility of the technique can provide great insights.

One that has proved to have a strong intuitive appeal is to identify a "disaster recovery program." Suppose you are modeling many thousands of scenarios for the first period in the model. Consider the 25 percent of scenarios under which the shortfall from your one-year goals is greatest. Under these scenarios, what is the average asset allocation that gives the best chance of achieving your goals at the end of the second period? This tells you, in advance, what action you ought to take if markets act against your best interests in the first period. This information greatly expands the knowledge of the decision makers and leads to greater confidence in adopting policies.

The more complex a model, the better its chances of taking into account the things that really matter. It forces you to consider your goals and fears in greater detail. This is a good thing, but it consumes much more time. Such models are also more difficult to design and operate.

PRUDENCE IS PROCESS

Treatments of asset allocation policy are usually highly mathematical. In this sense, we have not followed convention in this chapter. Instead, we have focused on the thought processes which governing fiduciaries need to master. As we have already asserted, the golden rule for governing fiduciaries is that "prudence is process." Good process is the heart of good asset allocation policy.

NOTES

1. For a more complete treatment of how different actuarial processes virtually predetermine the relative attractiveness of equities and long bonds, see "Asset Allocation by Surplus Optimization" by D. Don Ezra, *Financial Analysts Journal,* January–February 1991.

2. An excellent treatment of the impact of the sponsor's financial position on asset allocation choices is contained in "Asset Allocation and Funding Policy for Corporate-Sponsored Defined-Benefit Pension Plans" by Michael W. Peskin, the *Journal of Portfolio Management,* Winter 1997.

3. For the asymmetry of many goals, see Peskin, "Asset Allocation."

4. The developing field of "behavioral finance" deals with issues of this nature. See "Non, je ne regrette rien (No, I regret nothing)" by D. Don Ezra, Russell Consulting Conversation Piece #13, 1996, for a light treatment of the subject. "Behavioral Finance" (Association of Investment Management and Research, Charlottesville, VA, 1995) is an investment practitioner's introduction to the subject.

5. Fisher and Statman suggest that actual asset allocation policies differ from those that optimize financial and investment goals for the same reason that people do not live on optimal diets: They need a "palatability" goal, too, though it is not articulated. See "The Mean-Variance Optimization Puzzle" by Kenneth L. Fisher and Meir Statman, *Financial Analysts Journal,* July–August 1997.

   In similar vein, Jack Gray, head of Investment Solutions at AMP Investments Australia Limited, in correspondence with the authors, provides a possible explanation for the traditional American 60/40 allocation. Consider two goals: "Exceed a real return of 3 percent per annum over three years" and "avoid a negative return more frequently than one year in seven." If both these goals appeal to fiduciaries, but they cannot agree on the relative importance to give to each goal, Gray finds that the 60/40 allocation is extremely robust to small changes in the relative weights. Finding an allocation that satisfies multiple fiduciaries is another aspect of comfort that must be taken into account in practice.

6. See, for example, "We Are All Schumpeterians Now" and "Risk, Uncertainty and Pension Investing" by Keith P. Ambachtsheer, *Ambachtsheer Letter,* Nos. 133, 134, 1997, for a scenario-based analysis of U.S. capital market history and possible scenarios over the following four years.

7. "The Markowitz Optimization Enigma: Is 'Optimized' Optimal?" by Richard O. Michaud, *Financial Analysts Journal,* January–February 1989, explores error maximization and other features of the technique.

8. The conclusions are taken from an unpublished study, "Rebalancing," by Ralph Jackson and Howard M. Crane, of Frank Russell Company, Tacoma, WA.

10

Creating Value through Policy Implementation

A man should never be ashamed to own he has been in the wrong, which is but saying, in other words, that he is wiser today than he was yesterday.

—Alexander Pope

THREE CRITICAL IMPLEMENTATION ISSUES

The governing fiduciaries have learned and debated. They now have a mission statement and an asset allocation policy. For better or worse, most of the factors that will shape the fund's returns have been dealt with. All that remains is to implement the chosen policies: Get the money into the capital markets. Then monitor the fund's progress.

But for most fiduciaries, the fun is only just beginning. In many ways, this is the most interesting of the fiduciary roles, involving contact with fascinating and sometimes celebrated investment professionals. But the objective here is not entertainment. This is the "value creation" role stressed in Chapters 3 and 4, as it arises from day-to-day decisions. And because it arises from day-to-day decisions, it involves the managing fiduciaries rather than the governing fiduciaries.

In this chapter, we consider issues related to implementation of the asset allocation policy:

- What are the fundamental choices? We identify three: active or passive management, internal or external management, balanced or specialist mandates.
- Are decision rights clearly and sensibly defined?
- What do the best managing fiduciaries do?

Our discussion is based on the principles enunciated in Chapters 4, 5, and 6.

THE FUNDAMENTAL CHOICES

Once the asset allocation policy decision has been made, the implementation issues arise. The policy decision has been based on the most comfortable trade-off between the search for additional return and the avoidance of return uncertainty. The usual assumption implicit in this work is that investment markets for different asset classes are in equilibrium, and that the only reasonable way to expect a higher reward is to take on more risk. The first implementation decision then is: Should we stop there, or add to the potential reward and risk by seeking to exploit inefficiencies in some asset class markets? That is the active versus passive decision.

In whichever way this question is decided, people or firms must be hired to execute the decision. Should they be external agents, or should they be hired as employees of the sponsor of the pension plan?

And when they are hired, should they be hired as specialists, one to each asset class or style, or should some of them be given broad mandates across several asset classes?

One other issue arises too. Who should answer these questions?

ACTIVE OR PASSIVE MANAGEMENT?

The active versus passive issue can be thought of as a policy decision or an implementation decision.

As a policy decision, it would be made by the governing fiduciaries. If they decide to be entirely passive, implementation is relatively easy. If they decide to be at least partly active, one way to proceed would be to specify the amount of tracking error from active management that they are willing to tolerate. In this way, they treat the issue in a way parallel to the asset allocation decision, because they can combine the two types of decision into a single aggregated risk tolerance for the total fund. Then they can leave it to the managing fiduciaries to decide which asset classes give them the best chance of creating value by spending the permissible amount of tracking error.[1]

In practice, this elegant solution is rarely adopted. Instead, the active versus passive decision is made one asset class at a time by the governing fiduciaries, often on the advice of the managing fiduciary and a consultant.

Since prudence is process, it is important to develop a justifiable view on a number of issues and document them in support of the active versus passive decision.

Who are the stakeholders affected by the results of this decision? How much risk can they tolerate? What are our views on the efficiency or inefficiency of various markets or segments? Are we seeking to improve our RANVA by getting a high return or by reducing costs?

Once those questions are answered, the task of implementation begins. This involves an assessment of the candidates to manage the assets actively or passively: their investment and human processes, ways to combine them into asset class exposures that match the asset allocation policy, the search for economies of scale.

Then document it all, even if only briefly. This is tedious, but prudent, not only for the present, but also for two future purposes. One is that unless a decision is made for the right reasons, it will usually be unwound for the wrong reasons. The second is that the document forms an admirable piece of education for new governing and managing fiduciaries who were not there when original decisions were taken.

INTERNAL OR EXTERNAL MANAGEMENT?

Hiring people or firms to invest the fund in the markets is an implementation job. It is therefore the responsibility of the managing fiduciaries.

Sometimes others preempt a portion of that responsibility. Some corporate CEOs or CFOs say, "Investment management isn't the business we're in. I want the entire management of the fund outsourced." Others say, "It's useful to parts of our business, like investor relations or treasury, to have that expertise on staff. I want always to have a portion of the pension fund managed internally." By limiting the choice available to managing fiduciaries, they are confusing the interests of the sponsor and the fund's stakeholders. It is cleanest to leave these decisions entirely to managing fiduciaries.

The criteria that the best managing fiduciaries use relate to their search for RANVA. Am I looking for the greatest likelihood of adding value through active management? Am I seeking to keep passive implementation costs to a minimum? What are the implications for human backup or support staff? If I hire internal staff, will I have the courage (and freedom) to fire them as I would an external firm? Should I apply one approach to some asset classes or styles and the other approach for others?

It is easy to see how different managing fiduciaries, in different circumstances and with different personal experiences, can come to different conclusions. But whatever they conclude, the best will have a supportable rationale.

It is also interesting to note how national practices can be homogeneous, yet differ from the practices in other countries. For example, trustees of U.K. pension funds favor external investment managers. But the largest Dutch pension funds are mostly internally managed.

Whatever the route, it is important to define best professional standards, to be met by internal managers in the same way these standards are required of external managers.

BALANCED OR SPECIALIST MANDATES?

The debate on balanced versus specialist investment managers is purely an implementation issue. As such, it falls into the bailiwick of managing fiduciaries. This issue plagues managing fiduciaries far more than it ought to. In the United States, specialization is accepted as a fact. That doesn't stop fiduciaries from giving managers balanced mandates where they are considered appropriate. In other countries, discussion quickly generates more heat than light. The issue is really very simple and requires no studies.

Intuitively, as in other fields, investment specialization ought to result in superior skills. And therefore a series of specialist mandates ought to produce superior performance, if the managers are well selected. However, specialist mandates require more work on the part of the managing fiduciaries (or their staff). They need to manage the sum total of the mandates so that they accurately reflect the asset allocation and asset class exposures that the investment policy requires.

In contrast, with balanced mandates the suspicion is that no one manager is the best across every asset category. Performance ought not to be as good. However, the consolation is that, if the mandate is given to a manager with broad market exposures in each asset class, the managing fiduciaries need only monitor, not manage, compliance with policy.

Those are the essential differences between the two choices.[2] Sometimes fees also become an issue because managers may be willing to charge a lower combined fee for two or more specialist mandates than the aggregate of fees for specialist mandates.

THE BEST MANAGING FIDUCIARIES IN ACTION

When managing fiduciaries make decisions on hiring and firing investment managers, what do the best of them do? Essentially, six aspects characterize their behavior:

1. *They have clear mandates.* They know the policies that have already been decided. They know what their decision rights are. They know how they will be judged. Governing fiduciaries play a large role in the making of good managing fiduciaries. The best managing fiduciaries are comfortable with their mandate.

2. *They are aware of the dynamics of the marketplace.* They have supportable views about the inefficiency of particular markets and

about the prospect of finding active managers who will create value for them.

3. *They acknowledge that selecting superior active managers is an art, not a science.* Some fiduciaries like to select active managers by running statistical tests on past performance. The best fiduciaries know that this is futile. They know they are buying future performance, not past performance.[3] Some decision makers can't accept this and crave more certainty than investment markets offer. These fiduciaries may not be psychologically suited to the role they find themselves in.

4. *They are careful in how they classify managers.* They know that asset classes have different style segments. They do not compare managers who operate in different asset classes or different styles within an asset class. This is one of the two massive errors that many fiduciaries are prone to making. "Ranking lists" or "league tables" in newspapers and industry journals invariably compare managers with vastly different styles. The best and worst performing funds over any period are always those with extremely concentrated substyles and portfolios that just happen to hit a period when the market rewards them well or poorly. This is no reflection of the manager's skill. The same irrelevance can also show up when managers or consultants present return comparisons. The best managing fiduciaries are not deceived by such nonsense.

A corollary is that a manager's performance should be assessed against an appropriate benchmark. There may be an index for the substyle. Failing that, there may be a measurement service that shows the average return for a number of managers in the substyle. Failing that, there may be an index or an average return for the main style of which the substyle forms a part, but this is less satisfactory.

Again, both the press and commentators who should know better are guilty of misleading their readers. Pick up your favorite publication. Check how often every U.S. equity manager is compared with the S&P 500 Index. This index reflects the performance of the shares of the 500 largest companies in the country. Even large capitalization managers typically choose from the 1,000 largest companies. Consequently, almost every manager shows a strong small-company bias relative to the S&P 500 Index. When large companies are performing better than small companies, most managers are bound to underperform the S&P 500

Index. But this is invariably reported as a colossal failure of the investment management industry. Nonsense.

At the other extreme, there have been many well-meaning attempts to customize a benchmark for every manager, taking into account all the idiosyncrasies of the approach. Conceptually, this benchmark (the manager's "normal portfolio," as it is called) is the ideal. In practice, different consulting services come up with such different normal portfolios for the same manager that this clearly remains an art rather than a science. It reflects our earlier comment, that a complete written description of an active manager's approach is extraordinarily difficult to get right.

5. *They make sure that their total exposure to each asset class is balanced.* Ignoring this is the second massive error that managing fiduciaries are prone to making. Whether a fund has only one manager in an asset class, or several, all that counts is its total exposure to that asset class. It needs to be balanced. By "balanced" we mean that the total exposure reflects the aggregate characteristics of the asset class. For example, if the asset class is domestic equities, the fund's total exposure should not have any permanent bias, high or low, for its P/E ratio relative to the market, its dividend yield, its price-to-book-value ratio, and its exposure to different economic sectors. Occasional bets may be necessary if outperformance is the goal, but there should be no permanent bets in one consistent direction. Otherwise, the fiduciaries are making a permanent bet that a particular factor will always be favored. Yes, of course there is an exception to this rule. If you really want to bet on a particular factor, so be it. Make sure to document your reasons well. Make sure the bet is conscious, not unconscious.

Even the most sophisticated managing fiduciaries frequently contravene this rule. Mostly, it is because they select managers who, in their view, will add value in their area of specialization. Then they forget to hold at least a passive exposure to the areas in the asset class that are not covered by the specialists. For example, they have more money placed with value managers than with growth managers in domestic equity. Or their aggregate domestic bond exposure is shorter than the relevant bond benchmark portfolio. Or their aggregate nondomestic equity exposure consistently underweights Japan, relative to world market capitalization. These unconscious bets typically explain most of the difference between their own asset class returns and the asset class benchmark returns, rather than the skills or weaknesses of their active managers.

6. *If they invest in privately traded assets, they know the relevant issues.* The most important issue is to develop and maintain an in-house expertise, or to rely on an external adviser, because of the fundamental importance of selecting partnerships or funds-of-funds to invest in.

The next most important issue is the ability to negotiate fees. The interests of the pension fund and the general partner must be aligned. Lessons have been learned in the past and transformed into industry practice. No fees for finding a deal, otherwise the incentive is just to keep finding deals. Annual fees based on amounts drawn down, not on amounts committed or on appraised values. The carry is based on the total partnership portfolio, not on individual deals; otherwise there is no incentive to make the best of the deals turning sour. If the carry is paid while the partnership is in being and the cumulative return to date falls below the priority return, a "carveback" provision takes effect. And so on.

In addition, it is important to observe the marketplace and watch for whether soaring returns tempt new investors into the market, causing a glut of supplied funds and possibly an easier environment for general partners to price partnerships for their own benefit.

Finally, managing fiduciaries have to stay on top of the just-in-time financing used in this asset category. Cash flow management and commitment management are essential. Drawdowns are required from time to time. Distributions come back. Both these features mean that the actual exposure to the category is invariably much lower than the target commitment. Consequently, to maintain the target exposure, it is necessary to make commitments that exceed the target—and this can be worrying. The best managing fiduciaries have learned to make commitments opportunistically, no matter where they are relative to target.

CLEAR DELEGATION IS MOST IMPORTANT

Implementing asset allocation policy is a complex business. Even the best managing fiduciaries will not get everything right. These realities should not stop governing fiduciaries from clearly delegating the management and operations functions to those best equipped to carry them out. The research cited in Chapter 2 was very convincing about this point. Good organization performance depends on clear delegation within the organization.

NOTES

1. This is the approach adopted by the Ontario Teachers' Pension Plan Board, featured in Chapter 13.

2. Many managing fiduciaries call for studies to demonstrate the superiority of one system of mandates over the other. This is futile. Ask yourself what would be convincing evidence. Suppose we could identify some funds where nothing but specialist mandates were awarded, and others with nothing but balanced mandates. Assemble a comparison of their returns. If one set of returns totally dominated the other, so that the worst in one set was better than the best in the other set, that should do it. We have never seen such a result, in virtually any set of performance comparisons.

   Even if we had, we'd bet that some fiduciaries would argue that the data are contaminated. The test isn't a pure test of balanced versus specialist systems. It also reflects improperly applied mandates and poorly selected managers, not to mention just plain luck over a particular period. And they would be right.

   In practice the test is tougher than that. Even in the United States, that bastion of specialization, most managers are happy to accept balanced mandates. Many managers would therefore be included in both sets of the comparison. This would be bound to produce a huge amount of overlap between the results. And even in other countries, where balanced mandates predominate, many funds have some degree of specialization: foreign equities, perhaps, or real estate. Few funds are totally balanced. All results would have to be adjusted to remove the enormous differences caused by asset allocation policies. Above all, luck alone over any time period would dominate the residue of the results. Don't waste your time or money. You're bound to find two bands of substantially overlapping performance. Whichever bias you had before, you'll still have after the study. Make your decision simply on the basis of confidence in managers and the hands-on effort you're prepared to commit to.

3. See Chapter 5, note 5.

11

From Data to Information to Knowledge

What gets measured gets managed.

—Stern Stewart & Co.

WHAT GOVERNING FIDUCIARIES NEED TO KNOW

This chapter addresses a topic of vital importance to managing an excellent pension fund: the information needs of the governing fiduciaries.[1]

Decisions have been made and implemented. But the governing fiduciary's job never ends. Your ongoing responsibility is to know about the big picture at all times. How have we done? How are we positioned for the future? Are our decisions still valid, or does something need to be changed? Are we doing the job?

You will receive reports and will be offered an interpretation. Reports vary enormously in their content and quality. In this chapter, we show how reports can be kept relatively simple yet focused on the decisions you have made, so that you can tell exactly what impact your decisions have had. Leave the comprehensive reports for your managing fiduciaries to study. Your information should be brief enough to constitute knowledge.

Essentially, your reports must address three questions:

1. How have we done? In turn, this has two aspects:

   a. Where does benefit security stand? This is the fundamental issue connecting assets and liabilities.

   b. What value have our investment decisions created? In this context, we introduce a measure of value created: the risk-adjusted net value added (RANVA).

2. What is our current investment stance? (There is nothing you can do about the liabilities.)

3. Have we been procedurally prudent?

We next examine each of these questions.

WHERE DOES BENEFIT SECURITY STAND?

Table 11.1 shows that at the start of 1993, *Mid-West Resources* had $1 billion in its pension fund. Expressed in units of $1 million, it appears on the table as $1,000. Liabilities, measured as realistically as the actuary could, were $1,044. These numbers were filed with the supervisory authorities for funding purposes. No new valuation needed to be filed for a few years. While this valuation was based on market values of assets and best estimates of liabilities (i.e., "marked-to-market"), the actuary planned to use smoothed values in subsequent valuations.

Table 11.1   Measures of Benefit Security at Mid-West Resources
(All Figures in $ Millions, 1993)

	Assets	Liabilities	Surplus
1. Opening values (best estimates)	1,000	1,044	−44
2. Closing values (actuarially smoothed)	989	900	89
3. Closing values (best estimates)	1,048	1,081	−33

The year appeared to go well. The fund earned an investment return of 15.8 percent, measured at market values. This was well above the actuarially expected return of 8 percent. However, the actuary planned to credit only one-fifth of the excess return over 8 percent in performing funding calculations. The actuary also reported that the year produced other actuarial gains of $23. While interest rates had fallen (this was a large part of the reason for the excellent investment return), the actuary did not plan to change the liability valuation basis, since the fall in interest rates was only about 1 percent.

This smoothing of both assets and liabilities by the actuary resulted in a report that showed that the benefits were now fully funded at the close of the year. Nevertheless, the governing fiduciaries wanted to be assured that full funding was not simply an artifact of the actuarial methods and assumptions. They asked the actuary to report the market values of assets and the most realistic estimate of the liabilities. These new values showed the benefits to be less than fully funded, on a marked-to-market basis, as Table 11.1 shows.

There are two important points to be made here.

First, since the primary purpose of the pension fund is to provide benefit security for the plan members, it is incumbent on the governing fiduciaries to check periodically whether this is being achieved. It is not sufficient merely to look at asset values.

Second, governing fiduciaries should understand that, in reports filed for funding purposes, sponsors and actuaries typically do not measure assets at their market values, nor liabilities at their best estimates. Governing fiduciaries should therefore ask for a report of assets and liabilities measured using best estimates. The surplus position revealed by best estimates will typically be more volatile than smoothed values imply, and most groups find volatility uncomfortable. But there is little purpose served by looking only at smoothed values. Living with volatility is a requirement of a successful governing fiduciary.

The governing fiduciaries of Mid-West Resources actually called for a complete reconciliation of all the financial activities that had taken place in the fund during the year 1993. This included contributions, benefit payments, asset allocation policy decisions, active investment management decisions, actuarial gains and losses, and changes in best estimates of valuation assumptions. The story of what they got, how they reacted, and how their understanding gradually deepened, is told in the corporate case study in Chapter 14.

All the remaining financial analyses that governing fiduciaries are interested in concern the asset side only.

INTRODUCING RANVA

In Chapters 2 and 5, we introduced the concept of RANVA, or risk-adjusted net value added. There we simply presented the concept. We said that returns should be charged with the direct cost of fund management and also the indirect cost of the risk taken. The idea of netting investment management fees and other operation costs from the fund's gross return is traditionally accepted. But we added that excellence lies in getting a higher return than reasonable compensation for risk implies. If RANVA is positive, then it represents value truly created for the fund.

Now we discuss some of the measurement issues that arise.

The RANVA concepts presented here are not original, though they are only beginning to be applied to pension funds. They are based on a financial management system pioneered by the New York-based corporate advisory firm Stern Stewart & Co. They define "economic value added" (EVA) as "after-tax profit less the cost of the operation's total capital." We have adapted this idea to the management of pension funds by suggesting that the risk capital employed by a fund should earn a required rate of return that reflects the sponsor's cost of capital or risk tolerance.

An increasingly popular measure of the amount of capital at risk is "value at risk" (VAR). The essence of VAR in a pensions context is the maximum amount of the fund that could be lost over a given time period owing to adverse financial market or individual investment experience. In theory, this is the entire fund—but not in practice. The VAR is coming to be defined as a "two sigma" event (sigma meaning a standard deviation), representing the type of event that should occur no more often than one period out of twenty.

In the context of pension fund investing, we need to estimate two standard deviations of risk exposure in order to estimate the VAR that requires compensation. For example, if a fund's return has an annual standard deviation of 10 percent, then its VAR would be 20 percent. This roughly means that the amount of loss that might occur one year out of twenty is 20 percent of the fund.

We also need to state what rate of compensation is required for each of the types of risk taken on. This could be done by estimating how high a return might have been earned if that portion of the fund had been subjected to a different form of risk. Suppose we somehow arrive at the figure of 15 percent per annum as this alternative return. This then becomes the cost of risk capital.

Next we can calculate the fund's excess return required to compensate for undertaking this risk. In this example, it would be 15 percent on the 20 percent VAR, or 3 percent on the total fund. From this we can calculate the fund's EVA—or, as we call it in a pensions context, "risk-adjusted net value added" (RANVA). It would be the return earned, net of fees, and net of a further 3 percent representing the risk charge.

Table 11.2 shows how the calculation proceeds. We have given it the grand title "Aligning Mission and Measurement," for the following reason. As discussed in Chapter 7, the mission of a pension fund arises from its role as the independent source of benefit security and its potential further role as a source of economic advantage for the

Table 11.2 Aligning Mission and Measurement

	Gross fund return	(line 1)
Less	Risk-free return	(line 2)
Equals	Gross risk premium earned	(line 3)
Less	Operating costs	(line 4)
Equals	Net risk premium earned	(line 5)
Less	Cost of risk capital	(line 6)
Equals	Risk-adjusted net value added (RANVA)	(line 7)

sponsor. That is the overall mission of the whole pension system. What can we say about the investment mission of the governing board?

The investment mission of virtually every governing board should be to produce a positive RANVA. In the very few situations where the sponsor wants to take as little investment risk as is feasible, the investment mission of the board should be to produce the risk-free return at the lowest possible cost.

In Table 11.2, line 1 (the gross fund return) needs no further explanation.

The risk-free return (in line 2) is not obvious.

In the case of a defined benefit pension plan, it is ideally the return on the lowest risk portfolio, that is, the portfolio that most closely matches the liabilities. The composition of this portfolio would be estimated by matching the time profile and the inflation sensitivity of the liabilities with corresponding characteristics of assets. This would be a matter of judgment.

Similarly, with a cash balance plan, the risk-free return would come from the portfolio that most closely reproduces the return-crediting formula specified in the plan.

In a defined contribution plan (or—horror!—if the governing board decides that it wants to ignore the liabilities), the risk-free return will presumably be based on short-term government-guaranteed instruments.

Line 3 then follows.

Line 4, the operating costs, is seldom measured with precision. The pension system incurs a number of external costs, particularly when some of its activities are outsourced. These are easy to measure. The internal costs, particularly the cost of time spent supervising the system or investigating illiquid investments, are rarely separated systematically because they are incurred by people whose pension role is a part-time adjunct to their main business role. Often, therefore, operating costs are underestimated.[2]

Line 5 then follows.

Line 6 is difficult to estimate. We devote the next section of this chapter to it.

And line 7: This is what the creation of value really means for a governing board. We would like to call it "economic value added," because that is what it is. But Stern Stewart & Co. have already trademarked the name EVA, so, for lack of anything more creative at this point, we will call it "risk-adjusted net value added," or RANVA for short.

Every measurement system needs caveats before the results are interpreted. RANVA is no exception. It is a measurement system for people who would rather measure the right things imperfectly than measure the wrong things perfectly or measure nothing at all. In addition to the difficulties in measuring the risk-free rate, the operating costs, and the cost of risk capital, even the basic gross fund return has its problems. For example, some assets may have appraised rather than market values. Finally, RANVA is a new measure and few are yet familiar with its orders of magnitude.[3] Despite these caveats, we believe it is the most fundamental concept in pension fund investment.

RANVA can, in turn, be split into two components. One reflects the market risk assumed by the governing fiduciaries when they decide to adopt an asset allocation policy different from the lowest-risk portfolio. The other reflects the value created by the fund's managing fiduciaries in their implementation of the asset allocation policy, whether through active or passive management.

We show how to make the split into two components in the next section of this chapter.

The second, or implementation, component was mentioned in Chapter 2. There, we displayed a negative 0.3 percent value in Table 2.1. In Chapter 2, note 7, we also noted that in fact it averaged somewhere between 0.0 percent and a negative 0.6 percent per annum, depending on how one does the calculation, for 98 North American pension funds over the period 1992–1995. We explain the reason for the range at the end of the next section on page 141.

RANVA defines the investment value that is created, it defines the investment mission, and it defines excellence in pension fund investing.

What is your RANVA? Look at it over a period of years, to remove the random fluctuations that plague all series of returns. Express it in percentage terms, and even in a period of high returns its small size, and the possibility that it is in fact negative, may surprise and disappoint you. Express it in money terms, and it will wake you up.

CALCULATING RISK CHARGES

As explained earlier, a risk charge is the product of two quantities: the required rate of return for the risk taken, and the value at risk. We will consider each of these pieces separately.

The Required Rate of Compensation for Risk

In concept, this is most easily understood as the expected return from a different way of putting the capital at risk. What are other ways of getting risk exposure?

For a corporate sponsor, an obvious alternative is to invest in some new capital project. The marginal rate of return at which these projects become acceptable is thus one possible required rate of compensation for pension fund risk. (Both rates have to be adjusted for taxes. In North America, where corporations are taxed but pension funds are not, the net corporate rate would be used as the gross pension fund rate.)

For a government, the imputed social return on its projects could be used.

Trustees in a defined contribution plan where the entire fund is invested as a whole, without member choice, could use the return on whatever alternative use the average member might put the money to.

When considering the risk of active (rather than passive) management in a fund, fiduciaries could use the return that would have been earned if the risk had been taken via a more aggressive asset allocation policy.

The principle is simple. If I do not take this risk, what could be done with the money? Whatever risk I do take needs to overcome the return from the alternative use, or else why should I take the risk?

The Value at Risk in Asset Allocation and Implementation Policy

As noted earlier, the value at risk (VAR) is typically measured as two standard deviations of return exposure. That is the simple rule we follow here. It now becomes necessary to divide the return exposure between its asset allocation policy and implementation policy parts.

The return exposure itself is typically measured by looking back. While risk is by definition a forward-looking concept, in practice an accepted proxy is the actual standard deviation of the relevant return. We accept this convention, noting the caveat that it assumes consistent market behavior from the past to the future. Now we need to split the actual standard deviation between its asset allocation policy and implementation policy parts.

The asset allocation policy part is conceptually simple. Construct two hypothetical portfolios. One is reset to the fund's asset allocation policy in a manner consistent with the rebalancing policy adopted.[4] The second hypothetical portfolio is the minimum risk portfolio. In any period, the difference between the returns on these two portfolios is a measure of the mismatch risk implicit in the adopted asset allocation policy. Thus, over a number of periods, twice the standard deviation of this difference is the relevant VAR for asset allocation purposes.

Similarly, to calculate the VAR from active implementation of the policy, consider the difference between the fund's actual return in any period and the return from the hypothetical policy portfolio. This is a measure of the mismatch between the actual portfolio held and the passively implemented policy portfolio. Thus, over a number of periods, twice the standard deviation of this difference is the relevant VAR for implementation purposes. In practice, this is often a small number because, in most cases, active implementation adds little to the volatility of a fund's total return.

We may want to extend the concept of RANVA to each asset class in the fund and to each manager.

For each manager, the relevant VAR is twice the average "tracking error" of the manager's returns.[5]

For each asset class, the relevant VAR is twice the average tracking error for the asset class returns. This will be less than the weighted average of the managers' VARs because typically the tracking errors are far from perfectly correlated.

Similarly, the total fund's VAR from its implementation policy will be far less than the weighted average of its asset class VARs because the asset class tracking errors are far from perfectly correlated.[6]

We do not claim that these methods of estimating VAR are the only possible approach. We have seen other defensible ways of decomposing the total fund's actual volatility. The RANVA concept is so new that we would be pleased to see experiments in calculating RANVA. The concept itself is what we consider so very important.

To illustrate orders of magnitude, we show in Table 11.3 an example of how RANVA might have been calculated for one fund. The numbers themselves come from the database maintained by Cost Effectiveness Measurement, Inc., and represent the composite of 98 funds for which they had all the relevant data for the four-year period 1992–1995.

This composite fund required two hypothetical funds to be constructed, one representing the composite asset allocation policy, the other the composite lowest-risk portfolio that most closely matched the aggregate liability characteristics. These two hypothetical funds respectively earned 10.6 percent and 8.4 percent per annum, net of the fees that would have been paid for their passive management. Thus the net risk premium earned was 2.2 percent per annum.[7]

The volatility of the difference between the returns of the two hypothetical portfolios was 8.0 percent per annum. Thus the amount of the fund deemed to be at risk from the mismatch of asset allocation policy with the lowest-risk portfolio was twice 8.0 percent, or 16.0 percent.

Table 11.3 Average Ranva for One Fund, 1992–1995

Asset Allocation Policy Component		
	Gross policy return (less passive fees)	10.6%
Less:	Return for lowest-risk portfolio (less passive fees)	8.4%
Equals:	Net risk premium earned	2.2%
Less:	Risk capital charge (15% on 2 × 8.0%)	2.4%
Equals:	RANVA for asset allocation policy	−0.2%
Implementation Component		
	Gross total fund return (less active fees)	10.4%
Less:	Gross policy return (less passive fees)	10.6%
Equals:	Net risk premium earned	−0.2%
Less:	Risk capital charge (15% on 2 × 0.0%) or (15% on 2 × 2.0%)	0.0% to 0.6%
Equals:	RANVA for implementation	−0.2% to −0.8%

Source: "How All Pension Funds Should Be Measured," *The Ambachtsheer Letter,* No. 130, 1996.

Arbitrarily using a 15 percent required rate of compensation for this capital at risk (since this is close to the required return on new capital projects that many corporations in the United States use), we arrive at a risk capital charge of 2.4 percent. Over this period, therefore, the asset allocation policy RANVA was −0.2 percent per annum. Another way of looking at this is to say that the hypothetical corporation involved would have been marginally better off to have taken the risk in its main business, while matching pension fund assets as closely as possible to the liabilities over the four year period 1992–1995.

The implementation RANVA was calculated differently. As a lower bound, the excess of the fund's actual volatility over the volatility of the hypothetical policy portfolio was taken as the added volatility from implementation. As it happened, this was negative: The fund's volatility was less than that of the policy portfolio. Reluctant to proceed as if active implementation incurred no risk, we raised the VAR arbitrarily to zero. This meant we assessed no risk charge. Nevertheless, the fund's actual return, net of active management fees, was 0.2 percent per annum lower than the passively implemented policy return. Hence, the lower bound implementation RANVA was −0.2 percent per annum.

The upper bound of the implementation of RANVA was calculated by treating implementation risk as a "stand alone" risk. So now the full 2.0 percent tracking error is doubled to a 4.0 percent VAR, which in turn is charged the 15 percent required rate of compensation. An upper bound risk charge of 0.6 percent, and implementation RANVA of −0.8 percent results.[8]

OTHER REPRESENTATIONS OF RETURN

As stated earlier, few boards ask for RANVA calculations. Instead, the current state of the art revolves around two sets of presentations.

One is the comparison of performance against the backdrop of a sample of competitors or peers. This comparison starts with the total fund and proceeds through each of the asset classes and then each of the managers. Frequently the order is reversed, with more attention given to the managers than to the total fund.

The other is the attribution of the performance of the fund, or its asset classes or managers, to each of several levels of decisions or factors. Here comparisons against some backdrop are less frequent.

Both of these presentations provide insights, which is the main purpose of any analysis. Neither, however, provides the fundamental insights of the RANVA analysis.

COMPENSATION

We digress here briefly from this discussion of reports and measures that convey real meaning to the governing fiduciaries. Once one has calculated RANVA and appreciated its significance as true value creation for the stakeholders, there is an obvious application of the results. We have stressed how important it is for compensation to be aligned with the creation of value for stakeholders. The RANVA results are prime candidates on which to base the value-related, or incentive, component of compensation for those who have created value (regardless of whether they are internal staff or external suppliers).

WHAT IS OUR CURRENT INVESTMENT STANCE?

Governors should look not only at the past, but also at the future. Although they cannot tell what is going to happen in the capital markets, they should be aware of the departures the fund is currently making from its passive stance: the bets, essentially. Then, as market conditions develop, they will have a preliminary idea of whether the bets are paying off, long before they receive any reports.

Governors do not need to monitor daily positions. That is what the CEO and other managing fiduciaries do—as long as the ongoing monitoring task is assigned to someone who actually performs it. That is part of the intelligent delegation that is essential in every pension fund. Governors need to look only at the big picture, on a periodic basis.

With many large funds, governors look at the small picture on a quarterly basis. By "small picture," we mean a summary of the characteristics

Total Fund Asset Allocation			
Asset Class	Policy Exposure	Actual Exposure	Bet
U.S. Equities	50%	50%	0%
Non-U.S. Equities	20	21	1
Fixed Income	20	25	5
Real Estate	10	4	−6
	100%	100%	0%

U.S. Equities (vs. Russell 3000)		Non-U.S. Equities (vs. MSCI EAFE)		Fixed Income (vs. Lehman Aggregate)	
Cap Size	97%	Country Bets >	5%	Duration	−0.7 yrs
		United Kingdom	−10%		
Characteristics		Currency Bets >	5%	Major Market Bets >	10%
Price-to-book	104%	Not available		Cash	+16%
Dividend yield	88%			Treasury & agencies	−11%
LT growth forecast	113%	Cap Size	51%	Mortgage-related	−14%
Economic Sector Bets > 5%		Characteristics			
None		Price-to-book	98%		
		Dividend yield	93%		
		LT growth forecast	N/A		
		Economic Sector Bets > 5%			
		Financial services	−6%		

FIGURE 11.1 Fund Positions as of March 31, 1995. XYZ Pension Fund

of the holdings of every manager—and there are usually several. Usually much more time is spent on managers than on their aggregation into asset classes or into the ultimate aggregation, the total fund. This is the wrong way round. The big picture starts with the total fund. Then it reaches into the asset classes. Governors are wearing a managing fiduciary's hat if they choose to look at individual managers too.

There are many ways to show summaries of characteristics. Figure 11.1 is one possible way. It has the attractive quality of brevity, while providing considerable information.

- At the top of the summary is the fund's asset allocation. The adopted policy and the actual stance are shown. There is a bet against real estate and in favor of fixed income. Knowing how returns from real estate and fixed income develop over the next quarter, the governors will have an idea, before seeing reports, whether the fund is likely to have performed better than its policy or worse.

- The bottom half of the summary shows characteristics of the three largest asset classes. Each characteristic is measured against its passive benchmark, to show where the bets are. Thus, U.S. equities have a tiny bias away from large cap companies (the average capitalization of the holdings being 97 percent of the average capitalization of the holdings in the Russell 3000 Index^{SM}). This is so small that the relative performance of large and small companies in the next quarter will probably have little effect on the fund's U.S. equity return.

- A higher-than-index price-to-book ratio, lower dividend yield, and higher earnings growth forecast for the fund's holdings suggest that the fund is currently biased in favor of the growth style and away from the value style. Follow the financial press to see whether this current bet is paying off.

- None of the fund's economic sector weights differ from the corresponding index weights by more than 5 percent. There are, in effect, no noteworthy sector bets in the portfolio. Thus, in aggregate, the only noteworthy bet in the U.S. equity holdings is the growth bet.

- Similarly, the non-U.S. holdings have a country bet away from the United Kingdom and away from the financial services sector. In addition, the companies held in the portfolio are, on average, substantially smaller than those in the Morgan Stanley Capital International (MSCI) EAFE Index (which has a strong large-cap bias). Developments involving these characteristics are the only ones likely to have an impact on whether the asset class outperforms its benchmark.

- Under currency bets, the summary says "not available." Often currency bets are placed with overlays. Systems that capture the actual exposure of the fund to currency bets are hard to find.

- Finally, the fixed income portfolio has a short duration bet. This will pay off if interest rates rise, and will hurt if interest rates fall.

The high cash exposure is consistent with this bet. Both Treasuries and mortgage-related securities are underweighted.[9]

In this way, the governing board has a rough overview of where the fund's current bets are.

These summaries are difficult to produce. Everything starts with the underlying holdings of securities, derivatives, and other assets such as real estate. From the individual holdings, characteristics are compiled. Typically they are aggregated according to the manager portfolios in which they are held. Then they are aggregated into asset class portfolios, with some derivatives overriding the aggregation. Comparisons must be made with the asset class and total fund benchmarks in use. Then the summary in Figure 11.1 can be produced. It is essentially an "exception report": The only characteristics shown are those that are either routinely shown or that stand out by their size. And all this assumes the existence of adequate and acceptable sources of pricing, even for holdings that are traded infrequently in the marketplace or are one of a kind, like venture capital.

Ideally, one further stage of analysis would tie such a report back to the RANVA concept. The bets could be converted to VAR estimates, with all the caveats that forward-looking risk estimates require. Then the governors would have a feel for whether the active implementation bets are, in aggregate, higher or lower than the fund traditionally takes. This, too, is extremely difficult to do.[10]

Difficult . . . but so useful!

HAVE WE BEEN PROCEDURALLY PRUDENT?

You may have made excellent decisions without documenting them. You may have delegated responsibilities to others: Do you know whether they have been carried out? You may have ongoing responsibilities yourself that you have not carried out.

Checking these things is the final step.

Internal procedural audits are now being sought with increasing frequency by public sector plans and large American corporations. Using an external supplier of compliance and procedural audit services is sometimes done, too, again with public sector funds leading the way. It is human nature to think of this kind of check as dreary and tiresome. Yet when process is the essential component of prudence, it is a necessary final step.

NOTES

1. While this chapter focuses on the information needs of governing fiduciaries, managing and operating fiduciaries have information needs too. The needs at each level, from governing to managing to operating, involve more and more detail. Governing fiduciaries need only look at the main characteristics of each asset class of the fund. Managing fiduciaries need to look at the characteristics of each portfolio in each asset class; indeed, some want to look at the actual portfolio holdings. And operating fiduciaries need to look at the holdings in each portfolio they are responsible for, as well as information that tells them why other eligible securities are not included. This last category of information might include (1) return predictions for all eligible securities with measures of confidence attached to them, (2) a rebalancing mechanism that attempts to minimize implementation shortfall based on the predictions and capital market realities, (3) ex post facto measures of predictive accuracy and implementation shortfall, and (4) adjustments to expectations based on experience. There are information-related challenges at all fiduciary levels.

2. Difficulties in measuring operating costs are best understood by the participants in the annual survey conducted by Cost Effectiveness Measurement Inc. (CEM). This firm currently works with 278 pension funds around the world, including 182 U.S. funds, with an aggregate of $1.5 trillion in asset value.

3. The first published measures of RANVA for a group of pension funds and for the best and worst in the group appeared in "How All Pension Funds Should Be Measured" by Keith P. Ambachtsheer, *Ambachtsheer Letter,* No. 130, 1996.

4. In practice, this is too difficult a calculation, and the hypothetical portfolio is rebalanced annually, quarterly, or monthly, just as in performance attribution. The difference in the risk charge arising from this approximation is insignificant.

5. The tracking error is the amount by which the manager's return differs from the appropriate benchmark. The term is obviously derived from the context of index funds, for which any tracking error is a measure of the fund's failure to reproduce the index return. For an active manager, a departure from the index return is necessary if the manager is to beat the return. The error here is better termed a tracking deviation, but referring to error is now common practice. The average tracking error is the root-mean-square deviation of the manager's returns from the benchmark returns.

6. In using this system of calculating VARs, the total fund in effect gets credit for diversification within asset classes and across asset classes. Is that fair? Yes. Are managers penalized by their apparently large VARs while they are given none of the credit for diversification? No. Managers with limited mandates are not capable of affecting diversification beyond their mandates. Only those who are responsible for implementation policy can affect such diversification. Only their measures of VAR should be affected by it.

7. The average liability return was calculated by estimating the marked-to-market return on a zero default risk bond portfolio with a duration of 13 years, and an inflation sensitivity of 65 percent.

8. See note 6 for a rationale why it may make sense to do more than one implementation RANVA calculation. While from the total fund perspective it might be justified to set a low risk penalty for active management, this is not necessarily the case when using RANVA for incentive compensation or calculations at the asset class or individual portfolio levels.

9. The benchmark for the fixed income portion of the fund may well be customized to fit the plan's liability characteristics. If so, it will usually be longer than the benchmark shown here and might well include inflation-linked securities.

10. A number of pension funds, including Ontario Teachers' (see Chapter 13) and the Dutch civil service pension fund ABP, have begun to work on this challenge. See the article "ABP Adds Risk Software" in *Pensions & Investments,* Nov. 24, 1997, for a recent update on the status of total fund risk measurement implementation.

12
Managing Small
Pension Funds

Little goods, little care.

—Ancient Proverb

WHAT IS "SMALL"?

An essential message of this book is that pension funds are businesses that deserve full-time, professional management. This raises an important question. What if the fund is not big enough to be able to cost-justify full-time, professional management? This chapter examines that question and its implications.

The question immediately prompts another question. When is a fund too small to cost-justify full-time, professional management? We suggest a rule of thumb. The key is the cost justification of supporting a full-fledged internal managing fiduciary function. We see the minimum "critical mass" here as two people: a senior and a junior pension fund executive. Add in a support person, and such other essentials as rent, travel, and so on, and a minimum annual expense in the $400,000 area results.

When is that level of expense too high? Probably when it begins to represent more than 0.1 percent of fund value. The implication is that funds with less than $400 million in assets are "small" by this definition. The corollary is that funds with asset values greater than this can support a full-fledged, in-house managing fiduciary capability. In fact, our experience suggests such a capability only begins to appear when funds approach the $1 billion threshold. So in fact, even a $1 billion fund might be small by this second definition.

WHAT SMALL FUND FIDUCIARIES SHOULD NOT DO

The most important thing for the governing fiduciaries of small funds to realize is that they are subject to the same principles of pension economics, capital markets, and investment management services markets set out in Chapters 4, 5, and 6 as large funds. Also, they should be just as interested in creating value as large funds. What is different is that they don't have full-time, professional pension fund management to help them achieve it. Also, they face higher unit costs for such external services as investment management, custody, and consulting. In short, they suffer from the diseconomies of small scale.

The governing fiduciaries of many small funds ignore this reality. It is common practice for small fund fiduciaries to try to "part-time" their way to success, attempting to do the same things they see their large fund cousins doing. Probably the most common manifestation of part-timeism is for pension committees to take over the managing fiduciary function, and to get intimately involved in creating an active management function for the fund's assets. The implication is that investment manager hire-and-fire decisions are made by groups of people who are not very knowledgeable about how to do that well.

SMALL FUNDS CREATE LESS VALUE

The actual investment results of small funds bear out our concerns. The study on the performance of 98 North American pension funds, first cited in Chapter 2, took a look at the relationship between risk-adjusted net value added (RANVA) and a number of fund characteristics. The most predominant fund characteristic, which correlated with RANVA, was in fact fund size. Specifically, for every tenfold increase in fund size, RANVA improved by an average 0.4 percent per annum. Or stated differently, for every tenfold decrease in fund size, fund performance deteriorated by an average 0.4 percent per annum.[1] For example, $100 million funds underperformed $10 billion funds by an average of 0.8 percent per annum.

What caused this deterioration in performance as fund size decreased? Two factors contributed equally. About half of the deterioration was due to increasing unit costs, and the other half due to lower gross value added. The increase in unit costs can be partially explained by diseconomies of small scale. For example, smaller funds have higher external management fees than large funds, and do not manage assets internally. However, that is not the only explanation. Smaller funds on average also manage a much higher proportion of their assets actively.[2] This is not a scale phenomenon. It flows from presumably conscious decisions by small fund fiduciaries.

Did these conscious decisions in favor of greater active exposure pay off? No. As noted, gross value added for small funds was in fact on average lower than it was for large funds. Thus small funds paid more to get less.

BACK TO THE BASICS

These findings suggest that many small fund fiduciaries need to take a hard look at the principles set out in Chapters 4, 5, and 6. Put more bluntly, many need to be far clearer about what they know, and what they don't know.

Four principles are especially relevant to small fund fiduciaries:

1. *Economies of scale reduce operating costs.* Is there some way for small funds to benefit from the economies of large scale?

2. *Define what the creation of investment value means to you.* Do you really want the fund to be a distinct source of economic value, or are you just doing what everyone else is doing?

3. *Charge investment returns with the direct cost of management and the indirect cost of risk taken.* Are you applying this principle to the fund?

4. *Understand the biological/economic model of the market for investment management services.* Do you know where the external investment managers you employ fit into this model?

We conclude this chapter with some thoughts on the implications of these principles for small fund fiduciaries.

INDEXING

A fundamental principle of game theory is that the only way not to lose in games you can't win is not to play. The small pension fund application of this principle is to implement the chosen asset allocation policy passively. The passive segment of the market for investment management services is converging toward a small number of giant firms that benefit greatly from economies of scale. The result is predictable performance at very low implementation costs in the form of management fees and transaction costs. Many funds would create considerably more value with this option than they have in the past, or are likely to in the future with their current part-time approach to managing the fund.

OUTSOURCING THE MANAGING FIDUCIARY FUNCTION

The alternative to not playing is to improve the odds of winning. This means teaming up with an organization that has the resources to potentially add value after expense and risk charges. A number of organizations with broad investment manager research capabilities offer their services as managing fiduciaries. For success, this kind of arrangement must meet two requirements:

1. There must be absolute clarity between the respective roles of the fund's governing fiduciaries and the firm to which managing fiduciary duties are to be delegated.

2. The managing fiduciary must be successful in its manager research and implementation functions.

How do you find such an organization?

FINDING A SUCCESSFUL MANAGING FIDUCIARY

Success can never be guaranteed. However, small fund governing fiduciaries will need good answers to some critical questions if their decision to outsource the managing fiduciary function is to pay off:

- How well does the candidate firm understand the market for investment management services?
- How many investment managers does it research?
- What does it look for in a successful active manager? Does it look at the human side as well as those aspects that can easily be subjected to numerical analysis?
- Why, when, and how are managers terminated?
- Can the candidate firm demonstrate that its own economic interests are clearly aligned with those of the fund?
- Can the candidate firm demonstrate that it has been successful performing the managing fiduciary function in other situations? Does it measure the RANVA it has produced?
- Can the candidate firm demonstrate that it is committed to performing the managing fiduciary function over the long term?

An external managing fiduciary that scores well in responding to these questions is likely to produce more RANVA than the in-house part-time method.

NOTES

1. See Chapter 2, note 5.
2. For example, in the CEM database, 21 percent of U.S. total fund assets were passively managed on an equally weighted basis, but 31 percent on a dollar-weighted basis in 1996. The equivalent numbers for Canadian funds were 13 percent and 20 percent respectively. The implication is that larger funds make more extensive use of indexing than smaller funds. (Note that the CEM sample shows higher proportions of indexed U.S. assets than the comprehensive survey cited in Chapter 6, note 3.)

PART FOUR
EXCELLENCE
IN ACTION:

Four Case Studies

How do the principles and practices we set out in this book translate into real-world experience?

The four cases covered in this part of the book deal with all the important dimensions of pension fund management: governance and organizational design, funding and asset allocation policies, implementation, and measurement.

The focus is on "best practice."

Chapter 13. Excellence in Action: The Teachers' Pension Fund

Chapter 14. Excellence in Action: HiTechCo, Mid-West Resources Pension Fund, and the Yale University Investments Office

13

Excellence in Action: The Teachers' Pension Fund

> All in all, the Board is very pleased with the results being achieved by Plan management from the perspective of long-term investment returns, improved member services, the exercise of fiduciary duties, and the commitment to public accountability.[1]
>
> —C. Edward Medland, Chairperson
> Ontario Teachers' Pension Plan Board

ALL IN A WEEK'S WORK

It had been quite a week for Teachers' Pension Fund CEO Claude Lamoureux. Not only had the media featured the fund prominently as the financial partner in a $68 million management buyout of a major newspaper chain early in the week, but they had also trumpeted the $728,000 in total compensation he took home last year far and wide later in the week. What is going on here, the press wanted to know. A supposedly conservative pension fund doing risky private equity deals? The CEO of a public sector pension fund earning more than 10 times the average pay of the teachers he is serving? The sky is falling!

No, Lamoureux had patiently explained, the sky is not falling. When seen in their proper contexts, both news events make sense. For example, the fund's current target weighting for private equity investments is a modest 2 percent of total assets. However, when you're a $50 billion fund, that modest 2 percent adds up to $1 billion. Even then, the highly publicized $68 million management buyout is less than 7 percent of the target $1 billion private equity portfolio, and only slightly over 0.1 percent of total fund assets. As for his own compensation package, the $728,000 resulted naturally from two significant prior events. First, the Plan's governing fiduciaries decided to support a Plan management reward structure with a significant incentive compensation component tied to creating stakeholder value. And second, the Plan had in fact created significant value for stakeholders since the new governance structure was adopted in 1990.

ORIGINS OF AN EXCELLENT PENSION FUND

Had the press been more patient, Lamoureux would have told them the remarkable story of how Teachers' had been transformed from an arcane, inflexible, inefficient government agency to one of the world's top best-practices pension funds within a 10-year period. It all started in 1987, when Ontario's Premier David Peterson appointed Malcolm Rowan to head a task force to examine the economics of the major public sector retirement systems of Canada's largest province. Within a year, Rowan produced a remarkable document titled *In Whose Interest?*[2]

The report's title is significant. It signaled that Rowan understood the fundamental importance of pension deal clarity, and of aligning the economic interests of the stakeholders and of the governing, managing, and operating fiduciaries charged with furthering those economic interests. So, for example, the report insisted on upside/downside symmetry in financial gains and losses on the pension plan balance sheet. Thus, if the taxpayers fully underwrite experience losses, they should also fully benefit from experience gains. On the other hand, if a pension plan is a 50–50 partnership, this too should be reflected "in whose interest" the plan is managed.

Further, the report argued, public pension plans should be subject to the same financial and disclosure standards as corporate plans. Thus they should aim to become, and to remain fully funded. Investment policy and its implementation should reflect industry best practices. Investments should in no way be required to further specific public policy aims. Only the financial interests of plan stakeholders should be considered. Finally, public plans should be set up and governed as separate legal entities, with bylaws agreed on by the stakeholders. Changes in these bylaws should only be made with full agreement of the stakeholders.

TEACHERS' TAKES OFF

Taking the Rowan recommendations quite literally, the Ontario Teachers' Federation and the Government of Ontario hammered out a 50–50 partnership deal that was finalized in 1992. The new Plan organization actually commenced operations on January 1, 1990, with the government underwriting all risks until the 50–50 partnership was finalized. Each of the two partners nominated four Board members, with the resulting eight members collaborating to choose the Board's first Chair, former Bank of Canada Governor Gerald Bouey. Immediately, the new Board made a momentous decision. They would do everything in their power to attract the best management team possible to plan and manage the fund. A competitive and incentive-oriented compensation philosophy was to be a key dimension of the new organization. Figure 13.1 on page 160 provides a more detailed look at the blueprint for the new venture from a governance perspective.

The "blank piece of paper" status of the Plan got the attention of the then-CEO of Metropolitan Life Canada, Claude Lamoureux. He and the board reached an agreement, and soon the search was on for the Plan's Chief Investment Officer (CIO). The search ended quickly, with Bob Bertram, Assistant Treasurer and Pension Fund Manager at Alberta Government Telephones joining the fledgling Teachers' organization. With a $16 billion portfolio of nonmarketable provincial bonds, and no investment organization, Lamoureux and Bertram had their work cut out for them. Their priorities were clear. They needed a long-term asset allocation policy that matched the needs of the Plan stakeholders, and they needed an investment team to implement it.

Mandate: the Pension Plan Board is an independent corporation empowered by the Teachers' Pension Act to manage the pension fund and administer plan benefits. The Plan is sponsored by two partners: the Ontario Government and the Ontario Teachers' Federation. The 1992 agreement signed by both partners now provides for equal responsibility for plan losses, and equal sharing in plan gains. It also provides for a six-member partners' committee responsible for changes in plan design including contribution and benefit levels and for the appointment process for the corporation's board of governing fiduciaries (called directors). No member of the partners committee sits on the corporation's board.

The Board of Directors: the board of directors of the corporation is legally required to act independently of the two sponsoring partners, keeping only the best interests of Plan stakeholders in mind. Each partner names four directors and the partners together name the ninth director who shall be chair. The criteria for director selection focus on the relevance of the expertise and experience to the mandate of the corporation. No member of management is a director. The board is responsible for deciding asset mix policy, for establishing risk constraints, for articulating compensation policy, for selecting the chief executive officer, and for monitoring results vs. appropriate benchmarks and for valuation of the Plan.

Board Effectiveness and Independence: a comprehensive education program is provided for directors. Each director is appointed for a two-year term, up to a maximum of four consecutive terms. This allows the partners to consider the effectiveness of directors on a continuing basis. The board has direct collective access to outside advisors. Individual directors can engage an outside advisor, with approval of the chair, at the organization's expense in appropriate circumstances.

The Role of Management and Performance Measurement: Ongoing plan administration and fund management is delegated by the directors to the chief executive officer and staff. To ensure alignment of economic interests between plan stakeholders and management, management receives annual and long-term bonuses based on the achievement of pre-set performance targets approved by the directors. The directors require management to set annual corporate objectives and plans, as well as longer-term business strategies. These are required in both the benefit administration and fund management businesses.

Accountability and Disclosure: Plan stakeholders have a right to know how their contributions are spent and invested. Annual reports to stakeholders shall comply with the demanding disclosure requirements for publicly traded corporations. More frequent communications with plan members take place through newsletters, individualized benefit statements and counseling, focus groups, quality-of-service surveys, management presentations, and daily telephone access.

FIGURE 13.1   The Excellent Pension Fund Organization: A Governance Profile Of *Teachers' Pension Fund. Sources:* Ontario Teachers' Pension Plan Board Annual Report, Toronto, Ontario 1996; and interviews with the Board's managing fiduciaries.

TEACHERS' IN THE 1990s

A focused, knowledgeable Board helped them to quickly achieve both goals. The decision was taken to move the asset mix to two-thirds equities, one-third debt as quickly as was practical. The Board understood that with the entire starting 1990 fund in a $16 billion portfolio of long, mid-term, and short nonmarketable, fixed-rate government debentures against a $22 billion portfolio of pension liabilities that were of much longer duration and also fully inflation-indexed, special measures would be needed. Management proposed a massive swap program that would see a large part of the fixed rate debenture interest swapped to floating rate interest, which in turn would be swapped for returns on specified equity indexes. In large measure due to this strategy, bond exposure had shrunk from $16 billion to $12 billion by 1996, while domestic and foreign stock market exposure went from zero to $33 billion. A recent asset mix policy revision has pushed the equity-debt ratio target even higher to 75–25 percent.

While the swap program began to transform the asset mix, Lamoureux and Bertram set out to build a best-practice investment organization. Today that organization numbers 120 people, organized into a number of "businesses." Each of the businesses has its own operating team with its own budget, investment benchmark, and a risk exposure allocation. Within these constraints, each team is expected to produce value for the fund through internal management, external management, or some combination of the two. Incentive compensation is tied to the actual amount of value produced. Continuous value-at-risk monitoring ensures the integrity of all of the team-level investment programs and their consistent aggregation up into the total fund investment program. Figure 13.2 on page 162 pulls all these pension fund management and operations dimensions together.[3]

YES, VIRGINIA, BUT DOES IT WORK?

Designing the excellent pension fund organization is one thing, getting the desired results can be quite another. For Teachers', so far so good. Its latest annual report listed the following highlights:

Mission: to deliver defined pension benefits to 300,000 plan members at an acceptable cost, while minimizing the probability of contribution increases. Plan benefits have been costed at about 16% of pay on the assumption that plan assets earn a long term annual rate of return of 4.5% above the inflation rate.

Funding Policy: the current contribution rate is in fact 16% of pay, divided equally between active teachers and the government. The goal is to build and maintain a 15% to 20% excess of assets over liabilities measured on a best estimate basis as a contingency against future adverse experience.

Asset Mix Policy: the goal is to match assets with the size and structure of plan liabilities, which have duration of about 14 years, and are fully inflation-sensitive. Given the long duration of the liabilities and their high inflation-sensitivity, a high level of equity content is justified. The current target is 75% of the fund, with an allowable range of 70–80%. Equity investments, which have an average duration of about 15 years, will be diversified by type and region, as set out in the Statement of Investment Policies and Goals. The current allocation within the equity component of the fund is about 50% domestic stocks, 45% foreign stocks, and 5% real estate and private equity. Debt investments have target duration of 7 years. Plan asset and currency volatility exposures, as well as the plan's liquidity needs are monitored on a regular basis, using current 'best practice' investment and information technologies.

Investment Operations: the goal is to subject as much of the total fund to value-creating active management as can be justified, given the incremental costs and risks involved. The investment team of 120 people has a blend of specialties and experience, ranging from economics, to investment analysis and deal valuation, to financial derivatives, to accounting and risk measurement, and to information technology and policy compliance. The total fund is decomposed into a number of active management risk pools such as large and small capitalization, core and specialty domestic and foreign stocks. Other pools involve real estate, merchant banking, and bond portfolios. Each of the pools has its own dedicated management team, with a mandate to create value subject to cost and risk constraints.

Monitoring Risk and Results: each portfolio is monitored daily for risk exposure using 'value at risk' estimation techniques. Estimates at the individual portfolio level are aggregated up to the total fund level. Also, the return of each portfolio is monitored against that of an alternative benchmark portfolio, which represents broad market experience for that particular portfolio mandate. The total fund return is monitored against a composite benchmark portfolio, using the asset mix policy weights. The return of the composite benchmark portfolio is monitored against the 4.5% real return assumption used to cost and fund pension benefits. Operating costs are monitored at the individual portfolio level and aggregated up to the total fund level. Overall operational cost effectiveness is benchmarked against a selected peer group of pension funds through an independent measurement organization. Pension plan assets and liabilities are monitored quarterly on a comparable mark-to-market basis.

FIGURE 13.2   The Excellent Pension Fund Organization: Pension Fund Management And Operations At *Teachers' Pension Fund. Sources:* Ontario Teachers' Pension Board Annual Report, Toronto, Ontario 1996; and interviews with the Board's managing fiduciaries.

- A $1.2 billion surplus of plan assets over liabilities.

- A four-year excess return of 8.6 percent per annum over the 4.5 percent benchmark real return used to value pension benefits.

- Of the four-year excess return of 8.6 percent, 7.5 percent was due to the asset mix policy decision. Current asset mix policy is domestic equity 34 percent, foreign equity 36 percent, debt securities 25 percent, and real estate 5 percent.

- The remaining 1.1 percent excess return was due to the successful active management of fund assets. This incremental 1.1 percent per annum over the past four years adds up to an additional $1.4 billion of fund assets. The current active-passive split is 25–75 percent. The current internal-external split is 89–11 percent.

- Total fund operating costs over the previous year were $39.9 million, or 8.6 basis points of fund assets.

- On a peer-relative basis, an outside measurement agency reported that "our investment costs were lower than the other funds in our peer group, and our active management value-added higher."[4]

- Total previous year compensation of the CEO and the other four highest paid executives in the organization amounted to $2.6 million.

Win-win outcomes for all!

THE CHALLENGES AHEAD

Despite the excellent results achieved, both Chair Ted Medland and CEO Claude Lamoureux ended their annual report commentaries on a sobering note. Medland spoke to those who fear the rise of pension fund power. He asked annual report readers to note the emphasis the board placed on the accountability of Teachers' not only to its own stakeholders, but also to the community at large. For example, the board's decision to have the organization's disclosure standards comply with the standards set by securities regulators and stock exchanges was purely voluntary. There is no legal requirement to do this. Also, because the fund is an important investor in public financial markets, the board has authorized fund management to comment publicly on any issue related to the pension plan and its investments.

In this context, fund management has spoken out publicly against stock option proposals deemed excessively favorable to investee corporation managements, and also against "shareholder rights" plans that entrench current management and discourage unsolicited takeover offers. Finally, Medland remarked, those who accuse pension funds of encouraging corporate managements to lay off workers to boost short-term profits are misinformed. First, Teachers' itself has a very long planning horizon, permitting it to be a long-term, patient investor. Second, there is documented evidence that companies that pay attention to management/labor relations as well as direct and indirect employment growth, and that invest in research and development, product quality, and customer service, are most likely to create sustainable value for their shareholders.

Lamoureux cautioned Plan stakeholders not treat the results of the four years as normal. For example, the 7.5 percent per annum excess fund return due to the chosen asset mix policy is not sustainable over the long term. Meanwhile, Plan demographics will lead to significant growth in pensioners and benefit payments 15 years hence, making fund performance and the management of operating costs over the next 15 years especially critical. Further, the Plan does not operate in a political vacuum. Future government policies regarding retirement and retirement savings could impact Plan stakeholders and fund policies and operations. Government intentions regarding retirement-related tax policy and pension investment restrictions will need close monitoring.

CASE COMMENTARY: WHAT COULD GO WRONG?

Board Chair Medland and CEO Lamoureux are astute to focus their analyses on possible Achilles' heels facing the Teachers' organization. As its economic power grows, potshots from outsiders with their own agendas also will continue to grow. So they will continue to have to be clear about whose economic interests the Teachers' organization is there to enhance, and to show this is a win-win proposition for both insiders and outsiders.

Another potential Achilles' heel is future financial performance. While Lamoureux addressed the impossibility of continued double-digit capital markets returns, we can be sure that he also wonders how long his organization can continue to produce the excess returns relative to the policy benchmark achieved thus far. New directors will not necessarily be as qualified as retiring ones. Talented investment people are hard to retain in an industry as well rewarded as institutional investing. The multi-billion-dollar direct investment programs in real estate and merchant banking always carry the risk of loss and instant negative media coverage.

Significant challenges continue to lie ahead for Teachers' board and management team.

NOTES

1. Quote is from "The Chair's Report," page 5 of the *Ontario Teachers' Pension Plan Board Annual Report,* 1996. Much of the factual material in this chapter comes from this report.

2. *In Whose Interest?* was the title of a 1987 report produced by the Task Force on the Investment of Public Sector Pension Fund (Ontario), chaired by Malcolm Rowan. Now retired, Rowan held a number of senior positions in the Ontario government, including President of the Ontario Energy Corporation, Deputy Minister of Energy, and Deputy Secretary of the Cabinet. Both of the authors of this book were advisers to the Task Force.

3. Not mentioned in Figure 13.2 is that Teachers' is developing a new "Value at Risk (VAR) measurement system and an incentive compensation scheme based on the net return earned on VAR.

4. The 1996 *Annual Report* identifies Cost Effectiveness Measurement Inc. as the firm that conducted the peer-relative study for Teachers' of value produced versus the cost of production. The incremental four-year 1.1 percent per annum due to active management cited in the Annual Report cost about 0.1 percent per annum to produce in terms of investment expenses. Thus net value added was 1.0 percent. Also, the annual volatility of the active management return component was 0.8 percent, measured as a standard deviation. Using the Risk-Adjusted Net Value Added (RANVA) calculation

rationale laid out in Chapter 11, the implied four-year RANVA due to active management was 0.8 percent per annum on a "stand alone" basis, 1.0 percent per annum on a joint basis, with asset allocation risk and active management risk pooled together. On a $40 billion asset base, that translates to between $320 million and $400 million of risk-adjusted net value added per year.

14

Excellence in Action: HiTechCo, Mid-West Resources Pension Fund, and the Yale University Investments Office

The American cases described in this chapter are woven together but based on actual experience. As certain issues were unresolved at publication time, the actual names and numbers have been changed to maintain confidentiality.

—The authors

BIG PICTURE ISSUES: PURPOSE AND MISSION

In these days of mergers, acquisitions, divestitures, and breakups, strange things happen. The competition for jobs in the resulting corporate entities is fierce. Corporate cultures change. People are forced to reassess their positions, and many choose to seek opportunities elsewhere. The law of unforeseen consequences found HiTechCo (HTC) with an inherited multi-billion-dollar defined benefit pension fund, one of the largest in the United States, and nobody with any relevant experience left to run it.

The named fiduciary was the Pension Investment Committee, consisting of the Chief Executive Officer, the Chief Financial Officer, and the Treasurer. Their first interim decision was to make no changes in the way the pension fund was run. Then the Treasurer picked two highly intelligent, trusted, and open-minded subordinates, Pam and Sam, for a specific task. They were told to learn as much as they could in a month, talking to anyone they chose in the industry. At the end of that time, they were to make recommendations that the Treasurer could send to the Board of Directors for HTC's next Board Meeting.

Among the people they chose to talk to was a consulting firm, where they spent a whole day. Though by this time their minds were no longer blank slates, Pam and Sam told the consultants to proceed as if they were starting from scratch.

"What's the purpose of your fund?" asked a consultant. "Apart from the obvious one of providing benefit security."

"We're starting tactically, right in the middle of things," replied Pam. "We haven't reviewed the deep questions yet. Yes, the fund does cover the benefits: Actually, we're slightly overfunded. Nobody quite knows whether the fund ought to have any other purpose. In fact, nobody wants to deal with that question. It stays just beneath the surface. I'm glad you raised it, because I've felt it's important, but I can't answer it directly just yet."

Sam added, "We do have some instincts, though. Management time is our scarcest resource. Our corporate instinct is to outsource wherever possible, and I don't just mean the pension fund. I'd guess that we'd want to be passive investors. We're a high-tech company, and that's our business."

"Not a high-tech-plus-investment-management company?" persisted a consultant. "You don't feel that successful management of a very large pension fund could be a source of competitive advantage?"

"No," said Pam. "We want the fund to be competitive, but this isn't where we're going to show how much better we are than other high-tech companies. We just don't have the time to devote our energies to that."

"Right now," continued Sam, "I think one of the things in a paper you sent us for background reading really applies strongly to us. One of the possible mission statements in that paper was 'Don't screw up, and keep a low profile.' Frankly, that's how I'd define success for the fund."

So that was agreed as the starting point (though, of course, it would have to be expressed more elegantly when the time came).

In rapid-fire fashion, Pam and Sam named the issues they wanted to discuss. What should their internal organization be? How many people should they have? What should they look for in a new pension fund executive? Should they be active or passive? What asset allocation policy should they adopt? What should they do about their inherited 15 percent exposure to illiquid "alternative assets"?

Too many questions! To be able to feel that they were making some progress, and to take back something solid to digest later, they started to make lists.

FIDUCIARY ROLES

They liked the concept of governing, managing, and operating fiduciaries, so their first list was to itemize the respective responsibilities.

The governing fiduciaries were the Pension Investment Committee. Their role was to decide (in this case, confirm) the fund's mission and objectives. They would also decide or confirm the underlying investment philosophy or beliefs. And they would choose the fund's organizational setup from the alternatives that Pam and Sam would offer, including the decision rights that different people would have. It would be their responsibility to confirm the asset allocation policy, relevant time horizon, and appropriate asset classes. And the bottom-line metric for judging whether or not the fund was successful: RANVA had a conceptual appeal, but there wasn't time to get to the details of the calculations.

The managing fiduciaries were the fund's internal staff: nobody at present! The pension fund executive to be hired would effectively be the chief managing fiduciary, perhaps even the only one. What would the job be? They made a list.

- Make recommendations to the Committee.
- Prepare reports for the Committee.
- Take responsibility for liquidity management: coordinating contribution and benefit cash flow in and out of the fund and across investment managers.
- Rebalance the asset allocation, or hire a tactical manager to make asset allocation bets, depending on the Committee's beliefs.
- Take responsibility for determining the fund's investment structure, for hiring, monitoring, and firing managers, and for negotiating their fees.

The operating fiduciaries would be the actual day-to-day investment managers, and one or more custodians to be chosen or confirmed in their current positions.

Support staff might also encompass trust administration and other positions.

Pam and Sam both wondered, right away, whether the pension executive's job would attract serious players ("best of class," as they put it). They felt that the Committee's beliefs would severely restrict the officer's scope to make the kinds of decisions that these professionals enjoyed. They even wondered whether the job could be made more appealing by giving it more scope.

One of the consultants noted that the pension executive's role is, in some organizations, a career position, of importance in its own right. In others, it is a rotational position, occupied for a few years by an employee learning the corporate financial ropes. The pros and cons of defining the role at HTC in either of these fashions were then listed, with the proviso that the "career job" pros and cons often varied with the corporate situation and the person occupying that role. That was as far as Pam and Sam wanted to go on that issue. They would give it more thought before deciding how to deal with it, perhaps interview some pension officers in both types of situation to get their views. It was not a point that had arisen before that day.

ACTIVE, PASSIVE, INTERNAL, EXTERNAL

Then they listed the pros and cons of active management, just to be able to understand the issue better. They felt this was essential before they decided how to deal with their instinct that the Committee would, out of consistency with general corporate philosophy, prefer to be passive.

From this discussion arose two unexpected aspects. One was the compulsion Pam and Sam felt that a fund as large as theirs should not be entirely passive. They would reflect on this. Did they really have a deep-seated feeling that it would be a shame not to exploit some markets where they felt they could add RANVA? Or was it just maverick risk, the fear of being different from everyone else? They honestly didn't know. They decided to interview the one major fund known to be entirely passive: the one known maverick.

The other aspect was that they felt, at this point in their learning curve, out of their depth to decide what to do about the illiquid assets. Should they disengage gradually (and then who would make the decisions as to when to sell, how much, and at what price)? Or immediately (bringing its own complications)? Or should they maintain the exposure (which they felt was inconsistent with the likely mission statement and likely asset allocation policy of being similar to the asset allocation of their competitors)? The one thing they became sure of was that they needed to resolve this issue quickly. They were a major participant in a pool of illiquid assets whose manager had just lost a significant individual. The manager would not be able to hire a professional of comparable stature unless given an assurance that HTC would not pull out of the pool.

For the rest of the day they dealt only with the liquid asset classes, and tackled the problem of staffing levels. This they did by filling in the cells in a matrix. Across the top of a whiteboard they drew two columns: "Wholly Outsourced" and "Wholly Internal." Across the length of the board they drew three rows: "100 percent Passive," "25 percent active," and "50 percent active."

In each cell they wrote what would be the tasks to be done, the kinds of internal people or external firms that would have to be hired, and how

	Wholly Outsourced	Wholly Internal
100% Passive	***Outsource:*** Index fund management Custody Consultant for policy support Third party procedural audit ***Internal Staffing:*** *4 people:* 1 pension officer 1 trust administrator 2 reporting/compliance/oversight/backup	
75% Passive **25% Active**		
50% Passive **50% Active**		

FIGURE 14.1   HTC Pension Fund Staffing Models.

large the internal staff would need to be. Figure 14.1 shows the format they used. Again, the discussion revealed aspects that were unanticipated. For example, in what seemed to be the simplest cell to complete (wholly outsourced and 100 percent passive), they first cheerfully entered "one person, part-time." Then they realized that this would not be sufficient to prepare asset-liability studies internally, to be credible on the inputs into such studies, to monitor markets for changes that brought new questions (are the existing indices still appropriate? should the manager be permitted to use derivatives to reduce the cost of passive market exposure?), and so on. So they increased the number to two, arbitrarily.

Then a consultant suggested that they consider the "optics," or appearance, of the recommendation. How would the CEO or chief legal officer react to the recommendation of having only two people to supervise the activities of what was really one of the largest funds in the country? Might it be politic to recommend, say, four people? If management felt that two would be sufficient, let them say so. That would be preferable to having Pam and Sam pilloried for appearing to have ignored the fiduciary optics.

That was as far as the day's discussion went. Pam and Sam had made considerable progress on most of their issues, and several recommendations were taking shape in their minds. But nothing is ever cut and dried in this business. No decisions are obvious. At any rate, they were well on the way to building a rationale for whatever recommendations they would end up making. Just as important, they were building the foundation for an excellent pension investment program. The more excellent the program, the better its chance of surviving amid the turmoil and turnover as people and corporations change. Prudence is process.

WHERE DOES BENEFIT SECURITY STAND?

Among the defined benefit plan sponsors that Pam and Sam visited was Mid-West Resources (MWR). One of the reasons was that, like HTC, MWR was known to have substantially greater liabilities for their retirees than for their active members. The other reason was that MWR staff members had made a presentation at a conference that showed a different way of assessing their funded position. The presentation intrigued Pam and Sam, and they wanted a lot more background. They wanted to know, not just what the approach was, but how it had developed. What dead ends did MWR encounter? Did all the governing fiduciaries endorse it, or were there some doubters? Here's the story they heard.

At the start of 1993, MWR Pension Plan had $1 billion in its pension fund. We will express this in units of $1 million and so we will call it $1,000. Liabilities, measured as realistically as the actuary could, were $1,044. At the end of the year, assets were $1,048 and liabilities, again measured as realistically as possible, $1,081. The unfunded liability had fallen from $44 to $33, an improvement of $11. The funded ratio had risen from 96 percent to 97 percent. This happened even though interest rates had fallen through the year, and the end-of-year liabilities had had to be revalued at the lower rate then prevailing.

Table 14.1 Marked-to-Market Change in Pension Security at MWR, 1993 (All Figures in $ Millions)

	Assets	Liabilities	Surplus
1. Opening values	1,000	1,044	−44
2. Contributions and disbursements			
(a) Normal contributions for service in year	6	6	
(b) Benefit payments during year	−128	−128	
(c) Additional contribution for amortization of unfunded liability	20		20
Net contributions less disbursements	−102	−122	20
3. Investment return	150		150
4. Net actuarial gains and losses		−23	23
5. Revaluation of liabilities		181	−181
6. Closing values (may not add because of rounding)	1,048	1,081	−33

Table 14.1 shows the first step in the analysis that MWR eventually used.

The most upsetting feature was the revaluation of liabilities. Everything else looked good. A contribution of $20 had been made toward amortization of the unfunded liability. The investment return had been extremely favorable, at 15.8 percent. Translated into dollars it looked even better, and dwarfed the contributions. There had been net actuarial gains from mortality and other elements of the plan's experience that reduced the liability. Together, these would have placed the plan in an overall surplus position—finally!

The plan was in an odd position, in fact. MWR had shed many divisions of its business over the years, but had maintained the pension assets and liabilities of all its retirees. The liabilities were now roughly 90 percent for retirees and only 10 percent for actives. MWR itself, with corporate assets of roughly $1 billion, was no larger than its pension fund. Unwittingly, while divesting itself of many lines of business to focus on its core competencies, it had become a two-line company: its main enterprise and taking pension risk! It wanted to get out of the pension business and focus exclusively on its main enterprise, where its expertise lay. It had just started a defined contribution plan for all new active employees, and given its current employees the option of switching out of the defined benefit plan—an option the younger ones had elected. The DB plan was therefore closed to new entrants. The amortization payments really hurt. They were three times as large as the current service payments, a huge percentage of the payroll of the active employees still in the plan, and MWR looked forward eagerly to the day when they could cease.

The asset allocation policy the governing fiduciaries were moving toward for the DB plan was to invest in bonds that almost matched the length of the liabilities. Nevertheless, they thought it was a bad time to get fully out of equities, so the policy still reflected some equity exposure. All assets, both bonds and equities, were actively managed against market benchmarks for the equities and a long duration benchmark for the bonds.

That the liabilities had jumped so much in a year when the governing fiduciaries were celebrating their high investment return, and full funding had apparently arrived, was deeply disturbing. It took much discussion before they understood that the very feature that had caused the high return—the fall in interest rates—meant that more money was required to pay off the liabilities. They did not need to file a valuation report for another two years; but they had been hoping to file one at the end of 1993 showing a surplus and therefore no need for the company to make further amortization payments.

Now they realized that lines 3 and 5 in Table 14.1 arose from the same source. Further, in a year when bonds outperformed equities, their equity exposure had hurt them. If their policy had been to invest purely in a bond portfolio, as close as they could get to matching the length of the liabilities without investing in "strips" (i.e., bonds from which a dealer had separately sold the right to the interest payments, leaving the stripped maturity payments available separately), the benefits would have been fully funded by now. Although the company wanted to get out of the pension fund risk business, the equity exposure in the asset allocation policy was a mismatch that had kept them firmly in the business and had not paid off in 1993. Active management was another feature they had chosen that also kept them in the business. Fortunately, it paid off in 1993.

Table 14.2 shows the presentation that reflected this deeper understanding. Sections 3 and 4 were the key elements. There was no bond

Table 14.2 Marked-To-Market Change In Pension Security At MWR: A Deeper Understanding (All Figures in $ Millions)

	Assets	Liabilities	Surplus
1. Opening values	1,000	1,044	−44
2. Contributions and disbursements			
a. Normal contributions for service in year	6	6	
b. Benefit payments during year	−128	−128	
c. Additional contribution for amortization of unfunded liability	20		20
Net contributions less disbursements	−102	−122	20
3. Mismatch between asset benchmark and liabilities			
a. Return on lowest risk portfolio (100% long bonds)	172		
b. Change in liabilities due to revaluation		181	
c. Difference equals impact on surplus			−9
4. Impact of fiduciary decisions			
a. Selecting fund's actual asset allocation policy	−50		−50
b. Active management and other effects	28		28
Total impact of fiduciary decisions	−22		−22
5. Events and trends not anticipated by actuary		−23	23
6. Closing values (may not add because of rounding)	1,048	1,081	−33

portfolio (they ignored zero coupon bonds as too illiquid and subject to the dealer's credit risk) long enough to have matched the liabilities precisely, so there was no way the governing fiduciaries could have fully hedged the impact that falling interest rates had on the liabilities. But they could have come within $9 of it if they had taken themselves out of the pension risk business. Instead, the equity exposure in their policy cost them a further $50, offset by a gain of $28 caused by departures from a fully passive implementation of the policy. (They had already analyzed exactly how the active management gain had arisen. As with most governing fiduciaries, they looked at the assets long before liability values were available. Expressing the gains in millions of dollars, rather than in the traditional percentages and basis points, galvanized them into recognizing the importance of their decisions.)

Meanwhile, they understood that the investment return, originally stated simply as $150, was in fact composed of three parts:

- A "lowest risk portfolio" return of $172 that reflected no decision at all by the board.
- A negative impact of $50 that arose from the board's decision on asset allocation policy.
- A positive impact of $28 that arose from implementation of the policy.

Line 5 reflected a change in label. What was previously called "net actuarial gains and losses" now became "events and trends not anticipated by actuary." They understood that the actuary's assumptions on mortality, termination of employment, the ages at which active members would retire, and rates of salary increase were really best guesses about the future. In 1993, specific events and underlying trends that had not yet found their way into the actuarial assumptions had given the plan a $23 boost.

One governing fiduciary rejected the entire analysis. He said, with pride rather than apology, that he stopped following the explanation at a very early stage. He denounced the focus on highly volatile numbers, no matter how appealing market volatility might be to academics and consultants. He greatly preferred the long-term smoothing that the actuary introduced. Not only, he said, was this much more consistent with the long-term perspective that was required of him as a fiduciary; it also showed assets finally catching up with liabilities, which was what his instinct told him had actually occurred.

Despite the confidence with which the MWR staff had made their presentation at the public conference, they admitted to Pam and Sam that the governing fiduciaries were still debating which of the two perspectives was more useful. In the interests of harmony, they were exploring whether there were aspects of each that might be fruitfully combined. Or whether there were other aspects that neither provided. Meanwhile, the internal debate had put an effective stop to action.

Pam and Sam appreciated the candor of the briefing. They would learn that these behind-the-scenes briefings are often extremely candid. Partly, this is because professionals are simply proud of what they do, and enjoy explaining it to others. Partly, too, it is because those on the leading edge are eager to expose their ideas and actions to academics and practitioners, in order to gain support and acceptance. It is lonely being isolated, not to mention the threat to the careers of mavericks should things go wrong.

BACK TO ASSET ALLOCATION

Pam and Sam found themselves reopening a line of thought that they had considered closed. This was the fund's asset allocation policy. They had assumed, after talking to the consultants, that it was enough to mimic the allocation of their competitors. Now they encountered MWR, with a policy that focused heavily on fixed income because of the dominance of their retiree liabilities. While their own retiree situation was not as extreme as MWR's, shouldn't they check out whether they, too, should be closer to matching assets against liabilities?

They decided they would call for an asset/liability study. In principle, the issues were clear. The more their policy moved to fixed income, the lower the long-term return they could expect, hence the higher the cost to HTC. But fixed income would also reduce the gap between the rates of asset and liability growth. Thus HTC would be more certain of the cost each year.

What Pam and Sam (and, they suspected, the governing fiduciaries) had no idea about were the orders of magnitude involved. How much was the likely sacrifice in long-term return? How much would this raise the long-term cost? How volatile would the short-term contributions be, given the available actuarial smoothing techniques, if the typical equity-oriented policy were adopted? It was to get a feel for these orders of magnitude that the study was necessary. Then a business decision could be made.

Benefit security did not raise itself as an issue. Security would come from HTC's ongoing ability to make contributions and take investment risk in the fund. The benefits were currently fully funded, and HTC planned to preserve that status. Matching assets to liabilities would give the immediate impression of security, but that would be illusory in an ongoing plan. It might become more important, though, if HTC wound up the plan, because then the intention would be to make no further contributions. Then the assets would take on the role of underwriting the benefits. At that stage, one might prefer to ignore that matching is an imperfect tool and do the best that available assets in the investment market permit.

If contribution certainty was so important to HTC that it would be prepared to adopt a more defensive asset allocation policy than its competitors, another consideration became relevant. Many high-tech competitors simply used defined contribution plans. If contribution certainty could only be secured at the cost of a higher contribution rate than HTC's competitors used in their defined contribution plans, perhaps the ultimate solution for HTC was to switch to defined contribution. But that was a consideration for another time.

A TASTE OF YALE

In connection with their illiquid assets problem, Pam and Sam knew they should learn as much as possible from Yale University's experience.

Yale University is known as one of the most committed and successful investors in alternative assets, with 20 percent of its endowment (in 1995) allocated to private equity and another 20 percent in absolute return investments.[1] Yale's prestige, name, and long experience in private equity investing make it a very desirable client and allow it to invest in some well-regarded funds that might otherwise have been closed.

Yale's equivalent of managing fiduciaries, their Investments Office, places a premium on building long-term relationships with a limited number of premier organizations. Another key principle is to select organizations where the financial incentives are properly aligned. Yale believes that organizations affiliated with larger financial institutions are breeding grounds for conflicts of interest and lack of incentives for people actually doing the deals. Yale's ideal fee structure is for the private equity firm to just be able to cover its ongoing costs from the annual fees, earning essentially all its economic returns from the "carry" tied to investment performance. But this creates problems, because sometimes the best venture organizations won't reduce their annual management fees enough to satisfy Yale. Then the Investments Office has to decide whether to abstain from a commitment, or to go ahead anyway. An important aspect of their success, they believe, is the continuity of the team managing the private equity program. The two senior players have worked together for a decade.

The Investments Office feels there are important benefits to being in the private equity market at all times. If they decide not to invest with a top-tier firm merely because the market is overheated, they might not be able to persuade the organization to accept their money when later market conditions are more favorable. As the Investments Office concluded, if Yale were to alter its steady commitment to private equity and seek to time the market, top-tier firms "would not want Yale's unreliable money."

More food for thought for Pam and Sam. Their plates were overflowing. It was time to pick the most appealing morsels and digest them.

NOTE

1. This section is drawn from "Yale University Investments Office," Harvard Business School Case Study 9-296-040, copyright 1995 by the President and Fellows of Harvard College, prepared by Professors Josh Lerner and Jay Light. Used with permission.

PART FIVE
PENSION FUNDS IN THE TWENTY-FIRST CENTURY:

Three Critical Issues

Pension issues have become "main street" issues.

The visibility and importance of three such issues cannot help but grow.

1. A benefit formula and length of service have traditionally defined pensions. This traditional approach is now being questioned, and in some cases replaced by an approach which focuses on contributions, capital accumulation, and individual account ownership. Is one approach better than the other?

2. The subject of broke national pension schemes gets regular media attention. What does "broke" mean? What is the "fix"? Is there only one, or are there choices?

3. Another subject receiving increasing media attention is the growing economic power of pension funds. Are pension funds changing the nature of capitalism? Is this good or bad?

15

Defined Contribution Plans Are Different, but Are They Better?

By different methods different men excel; but where is he who does all things well?

—*Charles Churchill*
1731–1764

THE TROUBLE WITH DEFINED BENEFIT PLANS

When pension plans were originally designed, their goal was to reward workers who stayed with the same employer 25 years or more. So it was natural to define the pension earned in terms of a proportion of employee wages multiplied by the number of years worked. For example, a 1.5 percent per year pension benefit, multiplied by a 35-year working career, would result in a pension equal to 52.5 percent of annual earnings. Originally, the calculation was based on career average earnings. Increasingly, over time, it has come to be based on the average of the best or last few years of earnings, resulting in a more generous pension. So the traditional "defined benefit" (DB) pension plan was born and evolved.

Four fundamental factors caused some employers and employees in the developed economies to begin to question the value of the traditional DB pension plan in the 1980s:

1. As workforces became more mobile, and laws required shorter vesting periods, the "reward employees for long service" motive became increasingly tenuous. Thus quite naturally, pension vesting and portability have become issues. Associated with vesting and portability is the question of how the lump-sum value of the pension benefit accrues over an employee's working career, and who owns that lump sum. If this question is not addressed, it is quite likely that an employee who moves to a new employer every five years will, if each of those employers offers only the traditional DB plan as the pension benefit, end up with too small a pension on retirement. Quite correctly, mobile employees question the value of a traditional DB plan as the primary retirement vehicle. Some employers, too, have begun to question the importance of the "golden handcuffs" feature of DB plans as they redesign their compensation strategies. This questioning is reenforced by the fact that even very senior executives now consider themselves to be in the "highly mobile" category.

2. Quite apart from the economic value issue, the more educated segment of the workforce has come to insist on more personal control and transparency in its dealings with employers. The traditional DB plan does not score well by this count. It is usually controlled by the employer, not by plan members. Nor is the traditional DB plan very transparent. It is often cloaked in complicated financial statements and incomprehensible legal and actuarial language not understandable to the typical DB plan member. It is difficult to value something that is not understood.

3. As the traditional DB plan became a standard benefit with many large employers, governments became increasingly involved as legislators of pension laws, tax laws, and even divorce laws which touch pensions, and as regulators administering and interpreting those laws. Funding provisions, investment provisions, participation

provisions, vesting provisions, surplus ownership provisions, and tax deductibility provisions are just some of the myriad laws and interpretations of laws that this legislative and regulatory activity has spawned over the years in all the developed economies with substantial participation in DB pension arrangements. Quite predictably, employers have become increasingly sensitized to the administrative and compliance burdens and costs associated with sponsoring DB pension arrangements.

4. At the same time, smaller firms have become a more important segment of the employer sector in the developed economies, especially in North America. While large employers might put up with increasing DB plan-related administrative and compliance burdens, smaller employers cannot and will not. Not surprisingly, as the size of the firm decreases, the incidence of a DB plan as an employee benefit also decreases.

All these issues are relevant to employers in the developing economies, too. However, these employers often face additional hurdles. The technical and legal infrastructure needed to support the operation of DB pension plans may simply not exist. For example, an important component of managing DB arrangements is a professional cadre of qualified actuaries who can supply the necessary actuarial advice and services, and set out professional standards of conduct. It takes time to train and establish such a cadre, and currently it often simply does not exist. Also, DB plans need a robust, well-defined legal context. This, too, may simply not exist.

THE RISE OF DEFINED CONTRIBUTION PLANS

Given the circumstances surrounding traditional DB plans, it is not surprising that an alternate form of pension scheme began to emerge in the 1980s, both in North America and in some of the developing economies. In North America, DC plans have always been dominant among small employers. The passage of the Revenue Act of 1978, which created the 401(k) vehicle, was a major impetus to the growth of DC plans among larger U.S. firms.

In DC arrangements, the contribution rather than the pension benefit is defined. Thus now the employer agrees to contribute a defined percentage of the employee's wage into a designated retirement savings account. The contribution is invested in a guaranteed savings contract, or in a portfolio of financial securities. On retirement, the employee begins to draw down the accumulated financial assets in the retirement savings account, or buys a life annuity with the account's proceeds. Unfortunately, most employees withdraw the assets as a lump sum, defeating the plan's role as a provider of retirement income.

Despite this withdrawal risk, DC arrangements of this type appear to deal neatly with the four DB plan problems cited earlier. Now the pension savings account clearly belongs to the employee, and there is no surplus to argue over. If the employee moves on, the sum of accumulated retirement savings moves too. In most DC arrangements, the employee also has a good deal of control over how the money is invested. Financial statements provide a regular flow of information about the account's value and investment performance. Meanwhile, life has become a lot simpler from the employer's perspective. Much of the administrative complexity associated with sponsoring a traditional DB arrangement has vanished, although the golden handcuffs feature has too.

Finally, from a developing economy's perspective, DC arrangements mean being able to leapfrog many of the infrastructure issues associated with managing more complex DB arrangements. Thus in the developing economies, DC arrangements offer a less complicated route to making pension fund capitalism work.

THE CASE OF THE UNITED STATES

The Distribution of U.S. Retirement Assets

The history of the proportion of total retirement assets under employee control over the past 20 years in the U.S. private sector is traced by Figure 15.1. These assets include both those in some form of DC pension plan, and those in individual retirement savings (IRA) accounts. The proportion averaged about 20 percent of total private-sector retirement assets in the late 1970s, and rose steadily to about 50 percent in 1994, where it has

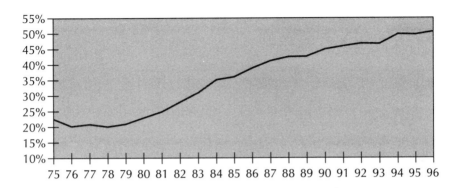

FIGURE 15.1   U.S. DC and IRA Assets as a Share of Private Sector Pension Assets. *Source:* U.S. Department of Labor, Employee Benefits Research Institute, Federal Reserve Board, and Sanford C. Bernstein & Co. estimates. This figure is reproduced from "The Future of Money Management in America," by Michael Goldstein, Jonathan Freedman, and Brian Bedell, Sanford C. Bernstein & Co., September 1996, page 14.

stayed for the past three years. Much of that growth resulted from the increasing popularity of the corporate 401(k) form of pension plan.[1] Table 15.1 shows total 401(k) assets in 1996 at $720 billion outstripped the combined assets of every other form of corporate DC plan.

Individual retirement accounts (IRAs) have also grown considerably, to an estimated value of $1.2 trillion in 1996. A major source of growth for IRAs has been rollovers from other forms of pension plans. A rollover occurs when a departing employee opts to move the accumulated value of DC plan assets or the commuted value of the accrued pension earned under a DB plan into an individual retirement account on a tax-free basis. Experts note that recent growth has come not so much from increased employee turnover, but from the fact that more employees now have larger amounts of pension assets vested. Tax law changes in 1986 and 1992 levied excise and withholding taxes on premature distributions of pension asset accumulations. The combined effect of these factors could see IRA assets continue to grow at rapid rates for years to come.[2]

Table 15.1 also outlines the rest of the U.S. pension assets picture. The $330 billion in DC assets under 403(b) plans relate to pension plans sponsored by not-for-profit employers such as private educational

Table 15.1   The Composition of U.S. Pension Assets in 1996

	Assets ($ billion)	Growth Rate 1991–1996E
401(k) plans	$ 720	17%
Other corporate defined contribution plans[1]	630	5%
403(b) plans	330	11%
457 plans	40	13%
Federal Thrift Savings Plan	30	NA
Subtotal corporate plans	$1,750	11%
Individual retirement accounts (IRA)	1,242	15%
Employee directed retirement accounts	$2,992	12%
Private and public defined benefit plans	$3,000	6%
Insured pension plans	1,140	15%

[1] Profit sharing, stock bonus, target benefit, and money purchase plans not organized in 401(k) form.
Source: U.S. Department of Labor, Federal Reserve Board, Employee Benefit Research Institute, Investment Company Institute, Internal Revenue Service and Sanford C. Bernstein & Co. estimates. Adapted from "The Future of Money Management in America" by Michael Goldstein, Jonathan Freedman, and Brian Bedell, Sanford C. Bernstein & Co., September 1996, page 41.

institutions, hospitals, and charitable institutions. The college employees' pension fund TIAA-CREF dominates this area with about 50 percent of total 403(b) plan assets under management.

The accumulated assets under government employee 457 and other thrift plans are much smaller at this time, at $70 billion, with $30 billion of them in the popular, passively managed Federal Thrift Savings Plan. However, proposals have been put forward in California, Michigan, and other states to permit state employees to shift from the traditional DB arrangements to new DC arrangements. If permitted, a new source of DC asset growth in the United States may have been uncovered. At $3 trillion, employee-directed U.S. pension assets equaled the value of the accumulated pension assets in corporate and public sector DB plans in 1996.

Current U.S. Issues Defined Contribution Plans

With the rapid growth in DC arrangements in the United States during the past 15 years, three broad and not totally unrelated issues have surfaced. They involve (1) participant choice of the appropriate contribution rate into the plan, of investment options available, and of services suppliers; (2) the need for and availability of participant education and advice; and (3) the potential for further coverage of the U.S. working population with DC plans.

Research confirms that generally, participants in DC plans in the United States have been making more informed choices with the passage of time. Employee participation rates where DC plans are offered have been rising. Contribution rates into DC plans by participating employees have been rising. Asset mix choices have become more balanced, with more money going into stocks and less into the traditional investment vehicle of choice, the guaranteed investment contract (GIC).[3]

Meanwhile, employers have been increasing their participant education efforts, and increasing the number of investment options for participants. Most large and mid-size employers in the United States now offer DC plans, most doing so alongside the traditional DB plan, rather than as a replacement for it. Table 15.2 shows that the 401(k) plan services suppliers of choice are the mutual fund groups, followed by insurance companies, and banks. The question of further coverage of the U.S. working population is largely a question of whether smaller employers will increase their efforts to offer and promote DC plans, with currently only 31 percent doing so.[4]

Table 15.2 The 401(k) Market: Investment Manager Asset Market Shares

	1988	1993	1997E
Mutual Fund Companies	14%	26%	43%
Insurance Companies	40%	34%	26%
Commercial Banks	31%	27%	22%
All Others	14%	13%	9%
Total	100%	100%	100%

Source: Investment Company Institute, Cerulli Associates and Access Research Inc., and Sanford C. Bernstein & Co. Reproduced from "The Future of Money Management in America" by Michael Goldstein, Jonathan Freedman, and Brian Bedell, Sanford C. Bernstein & Co., September 1996, page 43. Used with permission.

THE CASE OF AUSTRALIA

To secure the financial future of its citizens, Australia instituted a compulsory national DC-based retirement savings scheme with its Superannuation Guarantee legislation of 1992. The legislation mandates minimum employer contributions into qualified industry or corporate superannuation (i.e., pension) funds, reaching 9 percent of salary in 2002. Meanwhile, mandated employee contributions and government co-contributions have also been introduced. Combined, these contribution schemes will lead to a target 15 percent of pay total contribution rate by 2002.

Thus on the face of it, Australia has embraced pension fund capitalism with great gusto, with significant retirement savings cash flows into the 21st century a virtual certainty. However, a number of major issues remain unresolved:

- There continues to be a means-tested, pay-as-you-go Age Pension. In a recent brief to the government, the Institute of Actuaries of Australia has pointed out that means testing discourages retirement saving: the more you save for retirement, the lower your Age Pension will be. So why bother?[5]

- Further, pension savings accumulations have traditionally been paid out as lump sums in Australia rather than as lifetime pensions. Means testing encourages the quick spending of these lump sums in order to qualify for the Age Pension.

- The Australian retirement system is highly complex from a tax perspective, and not well understood by the population at large.

- Australian superannuation funds are governed by elected trustees, many of whom are not well versed in governing pension funds as financial businesses. This has led to an Australian pension industry that is highly consultant and money manager-driven.[6]

- While the issue of member choice on asset mix and investment funds has begun to be debated in Australia, the common practice of having only one fund in which all member accounts are invested continues. Further, there is often a discrepancy between a fund's market value, and the sum of participants' account balances. This results from attempts to smooth out market fluctuations and allocate smoothed returns to participant account balances. A recent government mandate requires that at least five investment choices be made available. This will likely accelerate movement toward member choice and market valuations.

Pension fund capitalism has taken off in Australia. However, for it to soar to great heights, a number of public policy, education, and industry structure issues still have to be addressed.

THE CASE OF CHILE

Chile became the first Western Hemisphere country to adopt an unfunded, pay-as-you-go national social security system, in 1924. It was also the first nation to privatize it in 1981. There were multiple reasons for the conversion. According to one analyst, these included the lack of relationship between premiums paid, inflation experience, and pension earned, as well as its ad hoc use as a social policy tool, and its gross administrative inefficiencies.[7]

As the old system began to break down, the bold decision was taken to terminate it and to begin a new private pension system based on compulsory pension contributions of at least 10 percent, up to a maximum of 20 percent of pay. The money was to go into new workers' retirement accounts to be managed by 12 newly formed private pension funds that had to compete for client business.

Outstanding obligations under the old system were retired through "retirement recognition bonds" that pay a 4 percent real rate of return, and that were deposited into each worker's personal retirement account. The Chilean government serviced this outstanding debt through budget surpluses and the sale of government assets. Those covered by the old system were permitted a choice between the old and new systems. On inception in 1981, 23 percent of those in the old system elected to move to the new one immediately. Today, only 7 percent of plan participants remain in the old system.[8]

The story of Chilean pension fund capitalism has been a good one thus far, carried by a 12 percent real return on pension fund assets until recently, with an average asset mix about 35 percent stocks and 65 percent in debt instruments. The happy combination of high returns and high contribution rates has been producing projected income replacement rates recently as high as 80 percent of average income during the past 10 working years. Meanwhile, Chile has sustained high rates of economic growth and developed its capital market infrastructure.

Not surprisingly, the Chilean pension model is being touted as the model all developing economies should adopt, and many are following in Chile's footsteps.[9] Indeed, the Chilean model is even being held up by some as the solution for the unfunded pay-as-you-go national pension schemes in the developed economies.[10]

However, one should not get too starry eyed. The Chilean system has yet to show its mettle in a low, or negative return environment. Investment choices continue to be limited, and foreign investments are still rare. Meanwhile, the commercial pension funds industry has adopted increasingly high-pressure sales tactics, as well as complex organizational and fee structures.[11]

Figure 15.2 shows that administrative expenditures were still a high 2 percent of assets in 1992.[12] While a 2 percent fee is bearable when assets earn a 12 percent real rate of return, it is not when capital market returns drop to more normal levels. Finally, few people have as yet

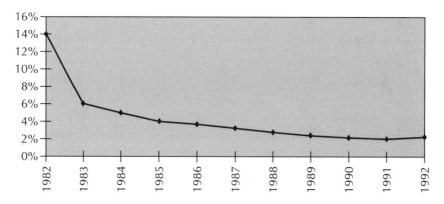

FIGURE 15.2 Relationship of Annual Administrative Expenditures to Total Pension Assets, Chile 1982–1992. *Source:* "Averting the Old Age Crisis," World Bank, Washington, DC, 1994.

actually retired under the new system. As is the case in Australia, pension fund capitalism is off the runway and into the air in Chile. However, crucial flight tests still lie ahead.

SO IS THE DC ROAD BETTER?

The building of the DC wave during the 1980s into the 1990s in such disparate places as the United States, Australia, and Chile raises the question of whether this form of pension arrangement will eventually become the dominant form for conducting pension fund capitalism. To come to such a conclusion requires the resolution of three further questions:

1. The rising tide of securities prices around the world during the 1980s into the 1990s has lifted all financial boats. How well will DC plan participants weather an extended spell of capital market turbulence sometime in the future?

2. Quite apart from any adverse reaction to future capital market turbulence, how well are DC plan participants equipped to convert a stream of working life retirement savings contributions into a predictable and adequate stream of postretirement pension payments?[13]

3. Who, if anybody, sponsors, manages, and underwrites DC retirement arrangements?

The answer to the first question cannot be known until an extended spell of capital markets turbulence has actually taken place. However, there is now a considerable "behavioral finance" literature that attempts to understand how people deal with making financial decisions under uncertainty.[14]

Two factors of that behavior stand out when tested. First, people generally suffer more pain from losing money than they experience pleasure from making it. Second, tolerance for risk taking is significantly influenced by the frequency with which portfolio results are calculated and communicated. Since portfolio results are communicated monthly, weekly, or even daily now in many DC plans, one cannot help but fear from these two findings that an extended spell of capital markets turbulence could lead to a sudden and precipitous drop in the popularity of DC plans.

DC Plans as Generators of Predictable and Adequate Pensions

There is more than meets the eye in the seemingly simple process of converting a stream of working life retirement savings contributions into a predictable and adequate stream of pension payments. Table 15.3 shows that behind the surface simplicity of a DC plan lie some difficult, but important concepts for people to grasp. The table sets out the relationship between pensions expressed as lifetime final earnings replacement percentages and investment returns under a certain set of assumptions.[15] These assumptions include a 35-year accumulation period from age 30 to age 65, a stable contribution rate of 10 percent of salary, salary growth averages 6 percent per annum, and the purchase of a single life, level pay annuity at age 65.

Under these assumptions, achieving a 4 percent return on assets yields only an 18 percent replacement rate of final earnings. Each 2 percent increment in assets returns increases the final earnings replacement rate by an improvement factor of 1.67, reaching a very attractive 83 percent replacement rate with an asset return of 10 percent. These results, and the relationship between them, help make four key points about DC plans as retirement income generators:

1. The ultimate pension produced by a DC plan is highly uncertain, with asset return experience a critically important variable. Low returns will lead to inadequate pensions.[16]

2. Asset returns and contribution rates are substitutes. Any target final earnings replacement rate (70% is a common target) can be achieved by some combination of a high asset return and a low contribution rate, or a low asset return and a high contribution rate. Unfortunately, by the time people discover that their actual contribution rate/asset return combination is not going to produce the pension they are targeting, it may be too late. Historically, for example, the turbulent 1930s and 1970s would have been difficult decades to exit out of DC plans into life annuities.[17] This may be

Table 15.3 Estimated Final Earnings Replacement Percentages under Three Return/Interest Rate Assumptions

Earnings Replacement	83%	50%	30%	18%
Return/Interest Rate	10%	8%	6%	4%
Other Key Assumptions	• Entry age is 30, retirement age is 65.			
	• Contribution rate is 10% of salary.			
	• Salary growth averages 6%.			
	• A single life, level pay annuity with a 10-year guarantee.			

Source: This table was produced from a TIAA-CREF software package "Tables of Planning and Growth" which the organization makes available to plan participants.

the greatest long-term danger associated with DC plans. Unless the aggregate asset allocation under DC plans reaches as high a risk exposure as DB plans currently have, sponsor contributions will be partly wasted, employees will have lower pensions than they expect, and society will be worse off. The need for education is vital.

3. The plan in this example doesn't offer any postretirement inflation protection, in the sense that the annuity priced in this example offers a level pay, fixed payment stream at age 65. Typically, insurance companies will not issue inflation-linked annuities unless financial markets offer inflation-linked bonds allowing them to hedge inflation risk. Again, the high inflation 1970s would have been devastating in this regard. It is noteworthy that a number of developed economy governments have begun to issue inflation-linked bonds in the 1980s and 1990s. If inflation-linked annuities are offered, they will initially replace a lower proportion of final earnings than a level payment annuity.

4. The investment and administrative costs of managing the DC plan matter a great deal. A large, dedicated $185 billion system such as Teachers Insurance and Annuity Association-College Retirement Equities Fund (TIAA-CREF) in the United States delivers all the necessary services to its members at fees as low as 0.3 percent of assets per year.[18] In contrast, a member of an American 401(k) plan serviced by a third-party commercial vendor could easily pay a fee of 1 percent of assets, or higher. In a world where future

Table 15.4   Average Mutual Fund Expense Ratios versus Performance

	Top Five Performing Funds Expense Ratios (basis points)	All Funds in Category Expense Ratios (basis points)	Top Five/All Funds Proportions (%)
Short Bonds (296 funds)	54	87	62
Intermediate Bonds (518 funds)	53	96	55
Long Bonds (219 funds)	64	107	60
Balanced (351 funds)	96	138	70
Income (183 funds)	78	130	60
Growth & Income (367 funds)	75	120	63
Long-term Growth (608 funds)	91	139	65
Aggressive Growth (370 funds)	102	155	66
Global Bonds (203 funds)	95	162	58
Global Equity (507 funds)	109	186	59

Source: KanonCarré (Boston) and Micropal, published in *Plan Sponsor* magazine, March 1995.

preexpense asset returns are likely to be in the single, rather than double digits, such differences in expense rates will eventually mean the difference between an adequate pension, and an inadequate one. Table 15.3 equates the loss of 1 percent per annum to plan expenses to a 20 percent reduction in the ultimate pension that can be financed. Meanwhile, the results displayed in Table 15.4 indicate that, on average, mutual funds with lower expense ratios produce better net returns than those with high expense ratios.[19] These results are consistent with the proposition that in generally efficient financial markets, risk-adjusted gross fund returns are similar. As a consequence, low-cost funds will generally produce higher risk-adjusted net returns than high-cost funds.

There is indeed more than meets the uninitiated eye in targeting and actually achieving predictable and adequate pensions through DC arrangements.

SPONSORING, MANAGING, AND UNDERWRITING DC PLANS

The preceding four key points cited make it clear that leaving employees to fend for themselves through DC pension arrangements is problematic.

Except for the small minority that happens to be well versed in pension finance and investments, DC participants would benefit greatly from DC plan sponsorship and management by organizations willing and capable of acting in the best interests of the participants in an expert manner. This is a tougher challenge than some DC plan sponsors realize.

We have already offered the 1.8 million member TIAA-CREF as an example of a dedicated expert organization, which has been the supplier of retirement planning, investment, and administrative services to the U.S. higher education community for over 75 years. Started after World War I to provide low-risk, low-cost, standard insurance and annuity contracts, TIAA began to offer direct equity investing through CREF in 1952. Today TIAA and CREF assets both exceed $90 billion, in 10 differing investment options. All assets are invested with an emphasis on low-cost, passive management.

A number of large U.S. corporate employers have followed a similar hands-on route in setting up DC plans for their employees in the 1980s, usually alongside the traditional DB plan already in place. Extensive in-house education programs were established, and continue to be improved. Intelligent investment choices were created for plan participants by in-house pension investment experts. By using the same investment management structures already in place to manage the DB assets, economies of scale were created, resulting in low unit costs for plan participants. Effective and efficient employer-controlled administration and communication processes were put in place, which continue to be improved over time.

Other U.S. corporate employers have chosen more hands-off routes. Some have done so by off-loading all DC plan management and administration to a single outside for-profit vendor such as a mutual fund group or insurance company. The plan participant then chooses his or her own mix of the supplier's investment funds. Others have gone even further by creating "windows" for plan participants to choose their own combination of mutual funds or even to build their own investment portfolio by buying individual securities through a self-directed investment account. While this is undoubtedly a good route for well-informed DC plan participants, for many others these arrangements create a problematic "asymmetric information" situation. When the sellers of a service know more about its true nature and value than the buyers, the buyers will generally end up paying more for the service than it is really worth.[19]

There is a certain irony in these developments. The hands-off route was motivated by the U.S. Department of Labor's issuance of ERISA's 404(c) regulations in late 1993. These regulations, in response to the financial failure of GIC provider Executive Life, are supposed to relieve DC plan sponsors from legal liability due to poor investment performance if the employer offers a sufficient latitude of investment choices. It is now becoming the view of at least some U.S. legal experts that, taken too far, the hands-off approach may well be creating the very legal exposure plan sponsors are seeking to avoid.[20]

This view is supported by recent developments in Great Britain. In 1988, the government there introduced new legislation permitting employees to opt out of the employer DB plan, and set up their own individual DC plan. A recent report in *The Times* estimates that over 500,000 people have since been wrongly advised to leave the employer's DB plan. To date, the British Securities and Investments Board (SIB) has only been able to deal with 1 percent of the claims arising out of this growing fiasco. Victims are now turning to the courts, as neither the financial services industry nor the employer community is willing to shoulder the blame.[21]

CASH-BALANCE PLANS: THE BETTER WAY?

So it is now clear that DB and DC plans both have their structural and legal strengths and weaknesses. Is there a way of shedding the weaknesses of both, and combining the strengths? Some pension experts believe that the "cash balance plan" may be the answer. In a short period of time, it has become, according to a recent *Fortune* magazine article "the retirement plan of the future," with the level of interest among Fortune 500 companies "feverish."[22] While there are many variations, the basic idea with this type of plan is to fuse the predictability features of the DB plan with the portability and ownership features of the DC plan.

Thus, for example, the employer contributes a minimum percentage of pay such as 6 percent into employees' retirement accounts and agrees to credit a certain minimum rate of interest such as the Treasury bill rate plus 1 percent on the accounts. It may, at its option, occasionally credit additional contributions and interest to the accounts. The accumulated value goes with employees if they leave the employer. Regular account

statements make the benefit highly visible. Should employees reach retirement age with the employer, they can opt for the standard life annuity
form of pension, or defer any pension payments until the money is
needed.

Meanwhile, the administration of the cash balance plan remains with
the employer. Given their simplicity, this can usually be accomplished at
lower unit costs than either DB or DC plans. Also there is a lower need to
educate and there is lower legal exposure in relation to DC plans. By retaining control over the investment policy and the investment management
structure of plan assets, the employer retains the option to manage the
pension fund as a financial business. It can choose to earn a target spread
over the interest rate it pays on employee account balances through its
asset mix policy and active management choices.

However, cash balance plans have their critics too. From the employees' perspective, they are essentially a DC plan earning a potentially
noncompetitive rate of return. So they may not produce an adequate income replacement rate on retirement. Also, because cash balance plans
are treated as DB plans for funding purposes, an employer can justify
having a pension fund with smaller assets than the sum of the participant account balances.[23]

FULLY INFORMED APPROACHES TO RETIREMENT FINANCING BEST

The message of this chapter is that fully informed approaches to delivering employee pensions offer the best hope. It is important to understand
that the traditional DB pension plan has serious drawbacks for a mobile
workforce. But as noted here, a stand-alone DC plan, though far better
than no pension plan at all, is no panacea either. Given these realities, it
is not surprising that enlightened large employers increasingly see the
value of offering DB-DC combinations, or some combined new form fus-
ing the best features of both together. Smaller employers, as they search
for the right mix of DC services providers, must not just focus on the investment options and record-keeping capabilities, but also on their cost.

At the end of the day, regardless of which pension creation strategy
is chosen, the need for cost-effective, plan-member-oriented delivery

structures comes through loud and clear. Successful pension fund capitalism cannot afford either to be inefficient, or to be managed more for the benefit of the suppliers than for the benefit of the customers.

NOTES

1. This type of U.S. plan derives its name from Section 401(k) of the Internal Revenue Code, which allows an employee to elect to have a portion of compensation contributed to a qualified retirement plan. Section 401(k) was added as part of the Revenue Act of 1978.

2. "The Future of Money Management in America" by Michael Goldstein, Jonathan Freedman, and Brian Bedell, Sanford C. Bernstein & Co., September 1996. The IRA growth estimate is from page 49.

3. The Employee Benefits Research Institute (EBRI) based in Washington, DC, has confirmed these positive trends in a number of their studies over the past few years. The New Jersey-based firm Buck Consultants reports similar results in its 1996 "401(k) Plan Survey" which covers 586 employers. Its key findings were (a) rising enrollment levels by eligible employees and (b) more aggressive asset allocation decisions.

4. The 31 percent figure is cited in EBRI Notes (Vol. 17, No. 12, December 1996), page 9. It is for employers with less than 100 workers.

5. "A Better Retirement Income Strategy for Australia," The Institute of Actuaries of Australia, April 1996. This paper was prepared by the Institute for the Australian Senate Select Committee on Superannuation.

6. A good example of what supplier dominance can lead to is the recent decision of the New South Wales State Government to sell the asset management arm of the A\$20 billion NSW Superannuation Fund to a Deutsche Bank subsidiary. The proceeds (reportedly in the A\$250 million area) no doubt looked well in the government accounts. Deutsche Bank gained immediate entry into the Australian investment management market. However, it is difficult to see how this decision was focused directly on the best interest of the Fund participants, unless the Trustees believe strongly that higher cost external management will produce better risk-adjusted net returns than lower cost internal management. Research from the database of Cost Effectiveness Measurement Inc. doesn't support this as a general proposition.

7. *Social Security Reform in Chile,* Luis Larrain, Instituto Libertad y Desarrollo, November 1995. This paper was presented at a pensions conference sponsored by the Fraser Institute, held in Toronto, Canada,

November 15, 1995. See also "Chilean Social Security Reform," EBRI Notes, August 1997.

8. From testimony presented to the U.S. Senate Committee on Banking, Housing, and Urban Affairs by Jose Piñera, President of the International Center for Pension Reform, June 25, 1997.

9. Most other Latin American countries have now adopted the Chilean model. It is also being studied by the Central and Eastern European countries as a quick way to introduce pension fund capitalism there.

10. Recent proposals to reform the U.S. Social Security System and the Canada Pension Plan have included the idea of individual retirement savings accounts. See Chapter 16 for more on this.

11. See page 20 of the Larrain paper (cited in note 7). The original Chilean 12 funds have now expanded to 25. Compensation arrangements are complex, based on front-end load fees rather than ongoing management fees. This structure misaligns the economic interests of fund participants and the owners of the management companies.

12. See Figure 15.2.

13. It should be noted that the equivalent conversion process in DB plans is not necessarily risk-free either, unless pension payments are fully indexed to the rate of inflation.

14. See, for example, Chapter 17 of *Against the Gods,* by Peter L. Bernstein, (New York: John Wiley & Sons, 1996) for a detailed discussion of how people deal with making financial decisions under uncertainty.

15. The table is extracted from an educational software package that TIAA-CREF provides its plan participants, titled "Tables of Planning and Growth."

16. Lower-than-expected returns would eventually impact DB plans as well. However, the impact would be more gradual, with the negative impact possibly shared by the plan sponsor and plan participants.

17. Real returns in the securities markets were close to zero or negative during most of these two periods. This implies retirement savings would have produced much lower income replacement rates than expected. This in sharp contrast to most of the 1980s and 1990s when securities markets offered high real rates of return.

18. TIAA-CREF announced fee reductions on its stock and bond funds in March 1996, with the new range a low of 0.29 percent for its money market and bond funds, to a high of 0.40 percent for its global equity fund.

19. The "asymmetric information" problem in the market for active management services derives from the fact that most of the sellers of these

services know that financial markets are generally efficient, making it very difficult to produce higher risk-adjusted gross returns than other funds. In contrast, most of the buyers believe that some fund managers are better than others and are prepared to pay superior managers higher fees. Research suggests many retail investors use recent historical performance to distinguish between superior and inferior mutual fund managers. See, for example, "The Market for Investment Management Services: Is It Rational?" Michael Berkowitz and Yehuda Kotowitz, *Canadian Investment Review* (Spring 1991). The problem is that short-term historical performance is a poor predictor of future performance in an efficient market. Thus higher fees end up generally not being rewarded by higher returns. In this sense, retail buyers of active management services are likely to pay too much for too little. The value to such a buyer of participating in a pension fund managed according to the principles set out in this book is that it eliminates the asymmetric information problem. Sophisticated pension fund managements know as much about financial markets as the sellers of active investment management services. See also the writings by Richard Ennis cited in Chapter 6.

20. The Committee on the Investment of Employee Benefit Assets (CIEBA) of the Financial Executives Institute (FEI) based in Washington, DC, devoted a large part of its 1996 annual meeting to this issue. CIEBA members voiced differing opinions on how hands-on or hands-off they should be with respect to their roles in sponsoring DC plans. Clarin Schwartz, VP & Consulting Attorney with Actuarial Sciences Associates, voiced the view that, were things to go wrong for any reason and lead to legal action by plan members, the courts would look very sympathetically at their claims. There is also evidence that this kind of "top up" risk remains in the new Australian DC regime, especially where union influence is strong.

21. "Onus of proof is thrown on to victims in £4 billion pensions scandal," Sara McConnell, *The Times,* London, November 16, 1996.

22. "How to Maximize Your Pension Payout," Eileen P. Gunn, *Fortune,* October 28, 1996.

23. This financial legerdemain is accomplished by using an actuarial discount rate higher than the rate used to credit participant account balances. The higher actuarial discount rate leads to a lower "liability" calculation than the accumulated value of participant plan balances.

16
Fixing "Broke" National Pension Schemes

The Council has not only been unable to agree on a plan, we have been unable to agree on the proper criteria to use in assessing [possible] plans.

—Prof. Edward Gramlich, Chair
The Advisory Council on Social Security
January 1997, Washington, DC

WHAT DOES "BROKE" MEAN?

The newspapers in the developed economies are full of stories about when their national pension schemes will be broke. The expression "ticking demographic time bomb" usually has a prominent place in these stories. The common problem behind all of these stories can be explained quite simply:[1]

- Compulsory national pension schemes were established earlier in this century to provide the working population with income replacement rates from 25 to 50 percent of the average industrial wage at a retirement age of 65.

- These schemes have been financed on a pay-as-you-go basis, with each working generation paying the pensions of the previous generation through a payroll withholding tax. Some of the schemes have charged a bit more to build up a financial reserve, usually borrowed back by the government against the issue of nonmarketable debentures.

- In their early years, these schemes seemed to work very well, effortlessly paying the promised pensions at apparently low contribution rates. This was partially because at inception, pay-go schemes have many contributors and few retirees.

- The other contributing factor to the perceived early successes of most national pay-go schemes were the economic conditions of the 1950s and 1960s. High productivity and real wage growth rates produced higher than expected contribution cash flows. Rather than investing this cash windfall, it was spent on improving plan benefits.

- All this began to change in the 1970s and 1980s, as the national plans began to mature, as productivity and real wage growth slowed, and as the combined consequences of the high post-World War II (but now falling) birth rates, and steadily climbing life expectancies began to sink in. Where once there were many contributors and few retirees, it was becoming increasingly clear that the combined falling birthrates and rising life expectancies were creating a future when the ratio of retirees to contributors would rise dramatically. To support this much larger cohort of retirees, contribution rates for the still-working population would also have to rise dramatically.

- The continuation of these trends into the 1990s, aided by the psychological shock of the leading edge of the "boomer" generation having their 50th birthdays, has now created an atmosphere of crisis surrounding pay-go national pension schemes. Where once contribution rates were so low as to be hardly noticeable, they are now high enough to be visible and to matter, and when the boomer generation begins to retire in 2010 and beyond, projected contribution rates soar to heights deemed by many to be unsustainable.

Thus it is important to understand that national pension schemes don't go broke because the assets backing accumulated pension promises run out. Pay-go schemes go broke when the current generation of working contributors refuses to pay the level of contributions required to pay the benefits promised.

HOW BAD IS IT REALLY?

A useful way to begin to assess how bad things really are is to calculate what it would take in terms of increased contribution rates to get future national pension scheme inflows and outgoes to match. The International Monetary Fund recently published its estimates of the increases required in eight developed economies, expressed as proportions of national gross domestic product (GDP).[2] Table 16.1 indicates contribution gaps as low as 0.1 percent of GDP for Great Britain, to as high as 3.4 percent of GDP for Germany. Note that, generally, the countries with the largest current contribution rates also have the largest contribution rate gaps.

Table 16.1 Contribution Gaps in Unfunded National Public Pension Schemes as a Percentage of Gross Domestic Product

Percentage of GDP	Projected Average Contribution 1995–2050	Sustainable* Contribution Rate 1995–2050	Contributions Gap	Effect on Gap of Retirement at age 67
Germany	10.3	13.7	3.4	−1.2
Japan	3.9	7.2	3.3	−1.6
France	12.1	15.4	3.3	−3.7
Italy	16.0	18.5	2.5	−5.7
Canada	3.8	5.8	2.0	−0.7
Sweden	7.1	8.0	0.9	−1.0
United States of America	4.7	5.5	0.8	−0.3
Great Britain	4.2	4.3	0.1	−1.1

*The rate that, if applied immediately, would eliminate the gap.
Source: "World Economic Outlook," International Monetary Fund, Washington, DC, May 1996.

At first glance, Table 16.1 would not appear to be conveying a situation of crisis proportions outside of Germany, France, and Italy where contribution rates are already very high, and need to go significantly higher. The table shows that in some countries, simply raising the age of pension eligibility to 67 would close the gap. However, such revisions to the pension deal are hard sells politically. Also, note that the "Sustainable Contribution Rate" is calculated on the assumption that it remains in place for 55 years, from 1995 to 2050. It follows that every year of delay in raising the contribution rate enough to close the gap, increases the magnitude of the raise required in subsequent years. It remains to be seen how quickly and resolutely the developed economies will deal with their national retirement scheme financing problems.

Matters, however, are more complicated than that. Two additional factors must be considered when judging whether the fiscal situations in which most developed economies find themselves today are in fact of crisis proportions. One of these factors is the visible public debt most of the developed economies have taken on over the course of the past 20 years due to running budgetary deficits. Simply put, taxes have been insufficient to cover current expenditures. The difference has been financed by a growing issuance of government bonds. The other factor is the projected growth in national resources that will have to be devoted to providing health care to aging populations. The same demographic arithmetic applies.

AN 82 PERCENT TAX RATE FOR FUTURE GENERATIONS?

As already noted, when the boomer generation begins to retire, the ratio of retirees to workers will rise sharply. These relatively fewer workers will have to finance not only the benefits offered under the national pension schemes, but those offered under the national health insurance schemes as well. What do all these accumulated public obligations add up to? In a pathbreaking 1994 paper titled "The United States' Fiscal and Savings Crises and Their Implications for the Baby Boom Generation," authors Alan Auerbach and Laurence Kotlikoff answer the question for the United States with an analytical approach called "generational accounting."[3] Generational accounting measures how much past, current, and future generations have paid, are paying, and will pay in net taxes over their working lives. Figure 16.1 shows the results of their calculations using the U.S. government's own long-term fiscal forecasts; it includes both Social Security and Medicare obligations.

Net tax rates increased steadily for the generations born between 1900 and 1960 from 23 to 36 percent of lifetime earnings. Since 1960, rates have stabilized, remaining at a projected 36 percent of lifetime earnings for the current generation, assuming no changes to the rules of the game. The calculations leave it up to future generations to balance the fiscal books. In other words, the calculations assume that the current rules of the Social Security and Medicare games stay in place for all those already born, and that future generations will have to pick up the tab. Figure 16.1 indicates that tab is the equivalent of an 82 percent lifetime net tax rate. This is equivalent to saying that, with the current rules of the game, the fiscal future of the United States does not work. And if this is so for the United States, it will be so for the other developed economies too.

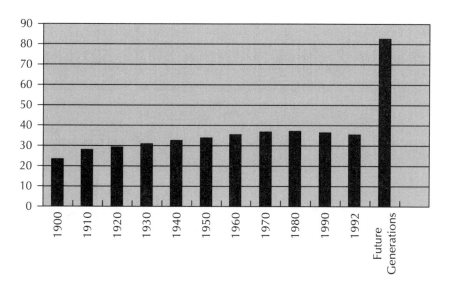

FIGURE 16.1 Lifetime Net Tax Rates of Current and Future Generations. *Source:* From "The United States' Fiscal and Savings Crises and Their Implications for the Baby Boom Generation" published in *Retirement in the Twenty-First Century—Ready or Not,* EBRI, Washington, DC, 1994. Alan J. and Laurence J. Ketlikoff, page 31.

CREATING FUTURES THAT WORK

Figure 16.1 offers a useful perspective on what must be done to make the fiscal futures of the developed economies work. The challenge is to create balances between public pensions, health care, and other government entitlements and services on the one hand, and viable and fair current and future net tax rates on the other. The devil in this challenge is of course in the detail. If there are to be cutbacks in government entitlements and services, on whom will they fall? If current workers are to pick up a more equitable share of the tab, how much more, and what is to be done with the additional contributions? Answering these questions in their broadest sense falls outside the scope of this book. Answering them in the context of creating viable national retirement financing strategies will be enough of a challenge.

Fortunately, we are not the first to take on this challenge. We have already cited the 1994 World Bank study on the coming old age crises on national pension schemes and its proposed responses to it.[4] Figure 16.2

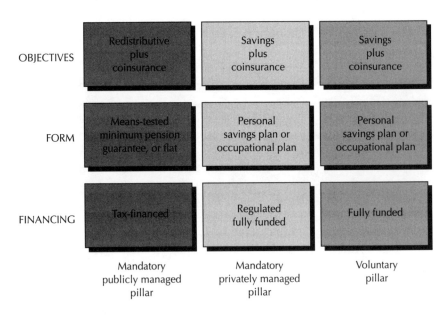

FIGURE 16.2 The Pillars of Old Age Income Security. *Source:* "Averting the Old Age Crisis," World Bank, Washington, DC, 1994.

summarizes the World Bank position. It proposes a three-pillar approach. The first pillar is a means-tested, tax-financed minimum pension guarantee. The third pillar is the voluntary private pension system. Most controversial is the middle "mandatory privately managed" pillar. We presented the Chilean and Australian versions of this middle pillar in Chapter 15. Great Britain began building its middle pillar indirectly in 1988 by permitting individuals and employers to opt out of the national pension plan. All three cases hold lessons for the other countries.

Where are the other major developed economies in terms of the World Bank three-pillar standard? Germany, France, and Italy have the furthest to go. They have very large unfunded second pillars and very little else. Recent measures have focused on incentives to strengthen the voluntary pillar. Japan, like Great Britain, also has a second pillar opt-out provision. However, its employment-based retirement system has suffered from the combined blights of many years of overregulation and underdisclosure, problems that Japan has only begun to address recently.[5] The United States and Canada have begun to address the second pillar issue only recently. We look at the progress they have made later in this chapter.

IS THE PREFUNDING OF PENSION OBLIGATIONS NECESSARILY A GOOD THING?

The most controversial aspect of the World Bank national pension model is its plan for minimizing the size of the universal pay-go first pillar through a compulsory fully funded second pillar. Income redistribution to alleviate poverty is contemplated only in the first pillar, and not in the second. The World Bank obviously believes prefunding pure pension schemes is a good thing. Nor are they alone. The idea that what ails national pension schemes in the world today can be solved by raising savings and investment rates has become a popular, widely held view. It is a central tenet of this book. We proponents of prefunding make the following argument to support our case:

- The least painful way of averting the coming aging crisis is to begin to raise societal wealth now.

- Additional wealth can only be created by raising savings and investment rates around the globe now.

- For this process to work, the additional savings must be invested through the financial markets, seeking the highest returns available.

- The government should have no say whatsoever in the disposition of the resulting pools of pension assets.

- The only legitimate role for governments in these new pension-financing arrangements is to ensure that they are operated in the best interests of pension plan participants.

While it is tempting to be so taken by this argument as to accept it as an immutable truth, this would be a mistake. There are credible commentators who find it all a bit too simplistic and facile. A number of commentators, for example, question who the asset accumulators will be 20 to 30 years hence when the funded pension plans in the developed economies hit their net divestment periods. Fortunately, the question has good answers.[6] The respected Wall Street economist and author Peter Bernstein, makes a more complete set of counterpoints to the immutable "truth":[7]

- Pensions are ultimately paid in cash, not in kind. This is as true for a prefunded pension system as it is for a pay-go system

- In both systems, pensions are transfer payments giving retirees a claim on current goods and services. In the first case, the payments are tax-financed. In the second case, they are financed by interest and dividend payments, and possibly the sale of securities. But at the end of the day, in either case it is tomorrow's working population that has to make the goods and deliver the services.

- Thus the crux of the matter is whether prefunding will somehow increase the size of the pie relative to its pay-go size.

- This is not at all a certain outcome. For example, tomorrow's high payoff investments may lie less in building new factories, and more in building human capital. Investing effectively in human capital is a much more complex proposition than simply putting money in the stock market. Meanwhile, raising savings will reduce consumption, which in turn could affect business investment plans adversely.

- Beware of apparently simple solutions to complex problems.

Taking the admonitions of Bernstein and others seriously, we take a more in-depth look at the prefunding issue.

THE ECONOMICS OF PREFUNDING

Four economists in Canada's federal Department of Finance took an in-depth look at the prefunding issue in 1995 in preparation for a review of the economics of the second pillar of Canada's retirement system, the mandatory pay-go Canada Pension Plan (CPP).[8] James, Matier, Sakhnini, and Sheikh began by observing that the economics of the CPP changed dramatically over the past 30 years. In 1966, the projected pay-go contribution rate in the year 2025 was 5.1 percent. Figure 16.3 shows why it

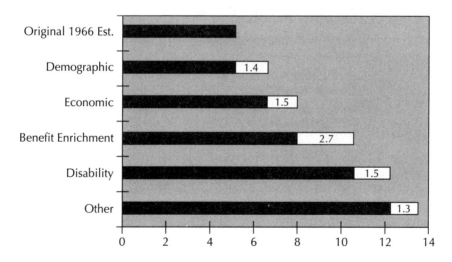

FIGURE 16.3 Projected CPP Contribution Rate in 2025: Cumulative Changes Between 1966 and 1996. *Source:* "The Economics of Canada Pension Plan Reforms," Working Paper, Department of Finance, Government of Canada, Ottawa 1995.

rose to 13.5 percent in 1996. It is instructive to understand why the best estimate 2025 contribution rate for the CPP has almost tripled over the past 30 years:

- Changes in demographic assumptions increased the contribution rate by 1.4 percent. This is the combined effect of underestimating life expectancy and overestimating birthrates.
- Changes in economic assumptions added a further 1.5 percent. This is the result of overestimating productivity and real wage growth.
- Benefit-related factors, including disability, added a whopping 4.2 percent.
- The reasons for the final 1.3 percent increment could not be clearly identified.

They observe that the material underestimation of the true cost of national pay-go pension systems 30 years ago demands that we reexamine their viability today. One of the key economic measures of the cost of pay-go systems is the gap between long-term real return prospects of pension funds and long-term real wage growth. In these systems, future benefit growth is determined by real wage growth; and once mature, this growth rate is effectively the internal rate of return on contributions. By contrast, the internal rate of return of a fully funded pension system is the return on pension assets. If this return exceeds real wage growth, prefunding will be cheaper than pay-go. Also, it will be actuarially fairer in the sense that all contributors now pay for their own pension during their working lives.

Once again, however, things are not that simple. There is an economic school of thought which asserts that increased national saving through prefunding national pension plan obligations will be fully offset by an equivalent decrease in private saving.[9] However, research by Feldstein and others on this issue suggests that indeed, there is some offset, but that it is considerably less than dollar-for-dollar.[10] In their economic simulations, James and coworkers conservatively assumed an 80 percent offset, pointing out that the lower the offset, the more powerful the economic impact of moving to full funding would be.

Using a fully integrated economic model of the Canadian economy and a series of assumptions about productivity growth, wage growth, and asset returns that they deem to be reasonable, James et al. simulated moving the Canada Pension Plan to full funding over a number of different time paths. They found:

- Achieving full funding involves temporarily speeding up CPP contribution rate increases above the projected pay-go increases. Estimating the potential benefits of moving to full funding must take this cost into account. The optimal path to full funding appears to be about a 40-year period.
- Despite the transitional costs of moving to full funding, the move produces a significant long-term gain in gross domestic product (GDP). Contributing factors are both lower distorting taxes and a higher savings rate. The former increases hours worked. The latter leads to a higher capital stock. Combined, they exert a powerful positive impact in GDP growth, even with the 80 percent offset in private savings they assumed.[11]
- A side benefit of the move to full funding is a reduced reliance on foreign savings, which in turn leads to lower levels of foreign indebtedness.

The authors of the CPP study stress that their results are suggestive only, based on the economics profession's best current understanding of how modern economies function. Such understandings are always considerably less than perfect. Also, they point out that they do not address the important question of how a move to full, or at least fuller, funding would impact financial markets and what kind of institutional arrangements would best facilitate the transition.

MOVING THE CANADA PENSION PLAN TO FULLER FUNDING: AGREEMENT REACHED

Using the CPP study as a point of departure, Canada's federal government issued a discussion paper on the CPP's problems and possible solutions in late 1995.[12] Two intergovernmental technical Working Groups were set up to study, and offer solutions to a series of implementation-related issues. Meanwhile, groups of elected Members of Parliament criss-crossed the country, holding public hearings on the discussion paper. By September 1996, these multiple processes coalesced to produce a political agreement on the following 10 principles:[13]

1. The CPP is a key pillar of Canada's retirement system and is worth preserving.

2. The CPP is a pension plan and will not be used to achieve income redistribution goals.

3. The redesign of the CPP must be fair across generations and between men and women.

4. Such fairness requires fuller funding, with the ultimate rate not to exceed 9.9 percent of pay.

5. Governments must tighten administration as a first step toward controlling costs.

6. While disability and survivor benefits are important components of the CPP, they must be contained so as not to jeopardize the security of retirement pensions.

7. Any further benefit improvements must be fully funded.

8. CPP funds must be invested in the best interests of plan members and maintain a proper balance between risk and reward. Governance structures must be created to ensure sound fund management.

9. The CPP must provide its members with a regular flow of understandable financial information about CPP assets and liabilities.

10. Governments must monitor the factors impacting the fairness and financial integrity of the CPP on a regular basis and be prepared to make whatever adjustments are necessary to maintain the preceding principles.

A key message of this book has been that acceptance of Principle 8, related to the investment goals and governance structure for pension assets, is fundamental to the effective operation of any pension plan.

We note with satisfaction that the Canadian government agrees. While some of the details about how Principle 8 is to be implemented still need to be worked out, a number of important decisions have already been agreed on. The CPP investment program is to be governed by a knowledgeable board of governing fiduciaries that will operate independent of government. The board will be bound by law to act in the best financial interests of CPP plan members, and will be accountable to them. It will be the board's responsibility to decide how to best implement its mandate.[14] It will be interesting to see if these good intentions will be followed through in practice.

MOVING THE U.S. SOCIAL SECURITY SYSTEM TO FULLER FUNDING: THE DEBATE CONTINUES

The United States has thus far chosen a different path to attempt to fix its Social Security system. Mindful of the political explosiveness of the issue, neither President Clinton nor challenger Robert Dole talked much about Social Security's looming financial problems, and what would have to be done to fix them, during the 1996 presidential election campaign. That task was left to the Administration's 13-member Advisory Council on Social Security. After two years of toiling, Council members have produced not one, not two, but three plans for public discussion. In its final report, they admit: "The Council has not only been unable to agree on a plan, we have been unable to agree on the proper criteria to use in assessing the plans."[15]

The fundamental disagreement among Council members revolves around Principles 1 and 2 in the Canadian agreement: whether Social Security is worth preserving as a mixture of an income redistribution mechanism and a national, universal defined benefit pension plan. Six of the Council members think it is, although like Canada, they are willing to contemplate higher contribution rates and an independently managed trust fund component to shore up its finances. The other seven want to make fundamental changes in the direction of establishing mandatory personal DC savings accounts, while maintaining a lower level of guaranteed pension benefits.

Where the seven Council members disagree is in how best to do that. Five want 40 percent of current payroll taxes to be redirected toward personal retirement accounts, with workers able to invest the money however they want. In their scenario, the $1.9 trillion unfunded obligations that would no longer be supported by payroll taxes would be financed by some combination of new Treasury borrowing and general tax increases. The other two Council members want to cut back Social Security benefits so that they can be financed by current contribution rates. However, an additional 1.6 percent would go into mandatory personal savings accounts. There would be a limited number of investment options managed by the Social Security system in this third scenario.[16]

A recent *Business Week* editorial summarized the current situation in the United States aptly with this title: "Entitlement Reform: A Bullet Not Bitten."[17] It argued that the time for councils, commissions, and task forces on Social Security is now over, and that the time for presidential leadership on this issue has arrived. Mr. Clinton's place in history could well hinge on how he and his administration deal with fixing the U.S. Social Security system.

No matter what specific solution is ultimately chosen, it cannot be successful without reliable mechanisms that cost-effectively convert retirement savings into additional national wealth. That in turn will require knowledgeable governance structures mandated to act in the best interests of plan members.

NOTES

1. The first part of this chapter closely follows Don Ezra's presentation "Demographic Trends and Capital Market Opportunities" to the World Affairs Council in Seattle, Washington, December 10, 1996.

2. "World Economic Outlook," International Monetary Fund, May 1996.

3. "The United States' Fiscal and Savings Crises and Their Implications for the Baby Boom Generation," by Alan J. Auerbach and Laurence J. Kotlikoff, was first presented at a policy forum sponsored by the Employee Benefit Research Institute (EBRI) in Washington DC, May 4, 1994. The research was sponsored by the EBRI Education and Research Fund. It was published in the 1994 EBRI-ERF book *Retirement in the 21st Century . . . Ready or Not.*

4. See Chapter 1, note 2.

5. See the article "Corporate Pension Funds: Senior Management Finally Takes Note," Masaharu Usuki, in *LTCBR Monthly,* July 1996, for a surprisingly frank discussion of the current state of pension governance, finance, and investments in Japan. *LTCBR Monthly* is published by the LTCBR Research Institute, a subsidiary of the Long Term Credit Bank of Japan, Tokyo.

6. Prof. John Shoven of Stanford University notes, for example, that the workforces of many developing economies are much younger than those of the developed economies. They will be net buyers of securities 20 to 30 years hence. Also, developed economy corporations can help facilitate the transition through stepping up share repurchase programs and dividend payments to shareholders. His comments are reported in "Demographics Is Destiny," *Strategic Economic Decisions* (Menlo Park, CA, November 1996).

7. *Social Security and National Saving: The Mantras and the Economics* by Peter L. Bernstein, Economics and Portfolio Strategy, October 1, 1996. This is a client publication published by Peter L. Bernstein Inc., New York.

8. *The Economics of Canada Pension Plan Reforms* by Steven James, Chris Matier, Humam Sakhnini, and Munir Sheikh, Working Paper, Department of Finance, Government of Canada, Ottawa, November 1995.

9. This issue of private savings offsets to increases in public savings has a long history in economic circles, going all the way back to the 19th century British economist David Ricardo. The offset concept, sometimes termed Ricardian Equivalence or full generational connectedness, was resurrected by Robert Barro in "Are Government Bonds Net Wealth?" *Journal of Political Economy* (November–December 1974).

10. "Social Security and Household Wealth Accumulation: New Micro Economic Evidence" by M. Feldstein and A. Pellechio, *Review of Economic Studies* (August 1979).

11. It is important to place the savings-to-investments conversion process assumed by the model in its current context. In the Summer 1996 issue of *Strategic Economic Decisions,* a quarterly advisory publication from Menlo Park, CA, financial economist Horace "Woody" Brock describes the modern four-stage process as (1) creative job destruction and re-creation, (2) high returns to innovation and innovators, (3) accelerating initial public offerings (IPO) activity, and (4) increased job creation.

12. *An Information Paper for Consultations on the Canada Pension Plan,* published jointly by the Federal, Provincial, and Territorial Governments of Canada, 1996.

13. The process of going from the 10 agreed-on principles to a detailed implementation plan was completed in December 1997.

14. One of this book's coauthors was asked to prepare a study for the Federal-Provincial Working Group on CPP Investment Policy on the best options available for creating an independent investment agency to invest CPP assets. "Moving to a 'Fiduciary' CPP Investment Policy: Two Possible Paths," by Keith P. Ambachtsheer, was first completed in June 1996 and revised in June 1997 for public distribution.

15. As quoted in the *New York Times* article "Panel in Discord on the Financing of Social Security" by Robert Pear, December 8, 1996. The formal report by the Advisory Council on Social Security to the President was released in Washington, DC, in June 1997.

16. Canada is adopting a governance model for its CPP Investment Board that is to operate independently of government. In the paper cited earlier (note 14), this choice was dubbed the "Independent Governance Model." This model is not being contemplated by any of the Council members. They see any market-based trust funds being managed passively by law on a predetermined formula basis. The proposed "Legislated Governance Model" reflects the fears many Americans continue to hold that, given the opportunity, politicians would meddle in the investment policies and operations of any Social Security trust funds.

17. "Entitlement Reform: A Bullet Not Bitten," Mike McNamee, *Business Week,* November 11, 1996.

17
Pension Funds, Politics, and Power

If pension funds do not belong to employees, to whom can they belong?

—Paul Harbrecht, SJ
Pension Funds and Economic Power, *1960*

YESTERDAY'S PENSION POWER VACUUM

Jesuit priest Paul Harbrecht may have been the first author who foresaw the questions related to political and economic power, which pension fund capitalism would eventually raise. His 1960 book *Pension Funds and Economic Power* argued that the growth in pension assets would occur in a power vacuum, unless some mechanism was devised to deal with the issue of pension asset ownership.[1]

His own view was quite clear. Pension assets belonged to plan members and should be managed in that context. He saw the coming accumulation of pension assets as an opportunity for workers to influence economic activity: "A voice in investment policy would allow the employees to help direct fund investments into channels beneficial to them. . . . "[2] However, he feared that such an outcome was unlikely for pension funds: "In fact, no-one owns them, although the prerogatives of ownership are being exercised by pension fund managers and financial institutions."[3]

Peter Drucker addressed the same pension fund capitalism power question 16 years later in his 1976 book *The Unseen Revolution—How Pension Fund Socialism Came to America*.[4] He, too, worried about the power vacuum being created by the continued growth of pension assets. He wondered whether pension funds would be able to withstand the natural tendencies of political processes to control and to use pension assets to further political goals. The best defense, Drucker argued, was to foster a sense of ownership of plan assets among plan participants. Like Harbrecht, he too recognized that this was problematical, especially in DB-oriented retirement systems.

As we do in this book, Drucker saw effective pension fund governance mechanisms peopled by knowledgeable fiduciaries as the answer. With effective governance, he argued, would come legitimacy. And with legitimacy would come the power to ward off illegitimate raids on the accumulated pension treasure troves. Further, Drucker argued such legitimacy would lead to the exercise of economic rather than legalistic prudence. In other words, "legitimate" pension fund governors would focus on genuine wealth creation goals rather than adopt rule-oriented "safety first" approaches to investing.

IS THE PENSION POWER VACUUM GONE NOW?

As the twenty-first century comes into view, the tremendous accumulation of pension assets foreseen by Harbrecht and Drucker has indeed occurred. Where Harbrecht cited a 1958 total U.S. pension assets figure of $100 billion, we cited in Chapter 1 an $8 trillion estimate for the year 2000, an 80-fold increase.[5] We have already noted that the United States has not been alone in accumulating pension assets. Increasingly, it has become a global phenomenon. What about the adverse consequences of the power vacuum Harbrecht and Drucker worried about? Has it materialized?

We would say "yes and no." Yes, there still is a power vacuum in the sense that for many pension funds, governance has still some way to go to meet the legitimacy standard Peter Drucker set for it over 20 years ago, and which we expand on in this book. The consequence, as pointed out earlier, is an excellence shortfall in pension fund returns, which may amount to as much as 50 basis points per annum in the average pension fund.

What has not materialized are massive raids on pension assets by pension system outsiders such as politicians or other power sources with possible ulterior motives. In this sense, Harbrecht and Drucker were unduly pessimistic in their predictions. The raids that have occurred have often been disguised and obfuscated, and have not caused major damage.[6]

The "economically targeted investments" (ETI) phenomenon to which the U.S. public funds in some states have been subjected to is a good case in point. The general idea with ETIs is to identify local companies, programs, or securities that for some reason are deemed not to get their fair share of attention from the financial markets or local funding agencies such as banks. State pension funds are then encouraged to fill the gap. While there is not a great deal of information available on the performance of ETI investments, what information does exist suggests that the realized rewards have not been commensurate with the risks taken.[7] Fortunately, little money appears to have gone into these investments.

This indirect kind of political raiding may have been more serious in other jurisdictions. For example, the giant Dutch civil service pension fund ABP has a long history of government-imposed constraints to how it could invest pension assets. As a result, its major asset categories for many years were low-yielding Dutch government bonds and residential mortgages. Interestingly, the Dutch government itself put an end to these practices through legislation in 1995. ABP's mandate now is to maximize value for its stakeholders, without any restrictions on how fund assets are to be invested. Table 17.1 sets out the remaining asset allocation restrictions placed on pension funds around the world in the mid-1990s.

RECEDING RESTRICTIONS

Table 17.1 confirms that the "overinvest in local government bonds/underinvest outside the country" theme still holds sway in a number of

Table 17.1   Government-Imposed Investment Restrictions on Pension Funds in 1995

Belgium	*Denmark*	*Japan*
>15% government bonds	> 60% government or like	< 30% equity
< 65% equities		< 20% property
		< 30% international
		> 50% principal guarantee
Canada	*France*	*South Africa*
< 20% international	< 65% equities	< 10% international**
	< 10% property	< 75% equity
		< 25% property
Chile	*Germany*	*Switzerland*
< 50% government paper	< 5% international*	< 30% foreign denominated
< 40% shares	(Pensionskassen)	< 50% total equities
< 12% international	< 30% equity	< 25% international equities
	< 25% property	

* <20% international for surplus portion.
** Possible through asset swaps.
Source: "The Global Pension Time Bomb and Its Capital Market Impact," copyright May 1997 by Goldman Sachs. Used with permission.

countries. That, however, is not the most important part of the government restrictions story. The most important aspect is that these restrictions have been steadily receding, as in the recent actions by the Dutch government regarding ABP. Until 1990, Canadian pension funds faced a 10 percent maximum limit on foreign investing. Industry pressure forced the Canadian government to raise it to 20 percent over a five-year period. Now that the new 20 percent ceiling has been reached, pressure is mounting once again to eliminate it completely. This will likely occur over the next few years.[8]

However, it is Japan that is experiencing the most dramatic easing of restrictions on pension investments. Until recently, the buildup of pension assets in Japan took place under highly restrictive conditions. The Japanese government has for many years mandated that pension liabilities should be calculated using a fixed 5.5 percent discount rate. It also mandated that only approved Japanese trust banks and insurance companies could manage pension assets, within the asset mix restrictions set out in Table 17.1. These arrangements created great pressure on these institutions to report pension asset returns in excess of 5.5 percent.

Aided by the high returns in the 1980s, as well as the ability to calculate asset returns on a book rather than market value basis, reported Japanese pension asset returns did indeed exceed 5.5 percent for many years. However, by the mid-1990s, just as the staggering pension liabilities facing Japanese society in the twenty-first century became highly visible, the reported returns on Japanese pension assets began to fall below 5.5 percent.

This experience triggered a major deregulation of the Japanese retirement system. Over a number of years, all investment restrictions are to be lifted, foreign firms are now allowed to compete in the pension asset management market, and asset returns will be calculated based on market rather than book values. An interesting consequence of these developments is that pension fund governance has recently become a topic of lively conversation in Japan. The move to deregulation provides important new incentives to pursue excellence, and to create value for stakeholders.[9]

BUILDING FIDUCIARY FRAMEWORKS FOR PENSION INVESTING

The developments in Japan are part of a global movement toward building fiduciary frameworks for pension investing. Fiduciary frameworks create legal structures that formally require governing, managing, and operating fiduciaries to act in the best collective interests of pension fund stakeholders. Probably the most influential of these frameworks has been the Employee Retirement Income Security Act (ERISA), enacted by the U.S. Congress in 1974.

The heart of ERISA is the legal requirement by the trustees of U.S. corporate pension funds to act solely in the best interests of fund stakeholders. The key ingredients of ERISA have been copied by many individual U.S. states in setting out their own legal framework for investing public sector pension assets at the state and municipal levels. Recently, the Management of Public Employee Retirement Systems Act (MPERSA) has been drawn up, which will formalize and standardize this process for public sector funds across the United States.[10]

How important was the enactment of ERISA in 1974? In their 1996 book on corporate governance titled *Watching the Watchers,* this is what Robert Monks and Nell Minow had to say about ERISA. They were commenting on the 1984 observation by Senator Jacob Javits, one of the principal authors of ERISA, that he had never anticipated the enormous effect ERISA would have on the direction capitalism would take in America:[11]

> What was unanticipated was the success of ERISA in combining an incentive for voluntary retirement savings with the power of compounding. . . . Suddenly, the law of trusts that was intended to define conduct for an infinitesimally small portion of GDP of 18th-century Great Britain was the informing energy underlying legal ownership of American industry. No one understood what they were doing. No one could anticipate the consequences.

So it was venerable English trust law, transported to the New World colonies centuries ago, which provided the missing link sought first by Harbrecht and then Drucker. It would be on the foundation of trust law that the era of pension fund capitalism would be built. Thus it should not be surprising that pension fund capitalism is most advanced in the United Kingdom, the United States, Canada, and Australia, developed countries where trust law has a long history. It is weakest in such countries as France and Italy, where trust law is a foreign concept.

THE GROWING INSTITUTIONAL OWNERSHIP OF CORPORATE AMERICA

When Harbrecht voiced his concerns in 1960 about pension funds as shareholders, the shares representing the ownership of corporate America were still largely in individual hands. Table 17.2, for example, shows the 1960 market value of all institutional equity holdings (i.e. pension funds, mutual funds, trust and insurance companies, etc.) at $52.9 billion, representing only 12.6 percent of total outstanding equities.

When Drucker added his voice in 1976, that percentage had doubled to 25 percent. Table 17.2 shows that by 1996, it had almost doubled again to 47 percent of total outstanding equity. Of that 47 percent, pension funds

Table 17.2   Institutional Holdings of Total U.S. Equity Outstanding

Year	Market Value of Total Outstanding Equity ($ billions)	Market Value of Total Institutional Equity Holdings ($ billions)	% Institutional Equity
1950	$ 142.7	8.7	6.1%
1960	421.2	52.9	12.6
1970	859.4	166.4	19.4
1980	1,534.7	519.9	33.9
1988	3,098.9	1,368.7	44.2
1989	3,809.7	1,710.7	44.9
1990	3,530.2	1,665.9	47.2
1991	4,863.6	2,065.5	42.5
1992	5,462.9	2,423.2	44.4
1993	6,278.5	2,909.4	46.3
1994	6,293.4	3,027.9	48.1
1995	8,345.4	3,889.5	46.6
2Q 1996 (P)	9,181.0	4,350.2	47.4

Source: "Institutional Investment Report," The Conference Board, New York, January 1997.

own 26 percent, mutual funds 12 percent, with the remaining 9 percent divided among trust companies, insurance companies, and foundations. However, the overall averages hide an important further fact. Of the 1,000 largest U.S. corporations, institutional ownership was up to 60 percent in 1996.[12]

The phenomenon of rising institutional ownership of corporate America has sparked a number of lively debates. Is institutional rather than individual ownership of the means of production in an economy good or bad? What does good or bad mean? How do you measure it? Not surprisingly, these debates focus on the existence or absence of economic power and how it is used. Their common starting point is usually the classic 1932 treatise by Berle and Means titled *The Modern Corporation and Private Property.*[13]

Berle and Means observed that the new technologies of the late 19th and early 20th centuries required capital resources not available to the individually and family-owned American corporations of the period. So they were forced to issue massive amounts of widely dispersed new equity through the securities markets to the American public. This issuance, combined with the advent of corporate mergers and professional management, led to a virtually complete separation of ownership from control in corporate America through most of the 20th century. Table 17.2 shows that this era is now coming to an end. A new era of pension-fund-led institutional equity ownership has dawned.

WILL AMERICAN PENSION FUNDS REUNITE OWNERSHIP AND CONTROL?

Berle and Means would have been happy with the advent of more concentrated, institutional ownership of corporate America. They believed that the complete separation of ownership and control was a bad thing. With that separation, they argued, came weakened accountability of boards of directors to shareholders, and weakened managerial incentives to create value for shareholders. Berle and Means would have seen large pension funds beginning to fill the power vacuum they worried about as a good thing. In *Watching the Watchers,* Monks and Minow document the evolution of this process from the mid-1980s to the present.

While Monks and Minow continue to have some concerns about the current effectiveness of pension fund governance itself (as we do in this book), they observe pension funds have the potential to be effective corporate owners:[14]

- Pension funds have the size and sophistication to make the monitoring of the effectiveness of boards of directors of investee corporations an economically rational proposition. This economic motivation increases as the potential gains from active trading decrease with asset growth.

- Pension funds represent the legitimate economic interests of millions of stakeholders.

- Pension funds are less restricted by commercial conflicts to play a monitoring role as are other institutional investors such as mutual funds, banks, and insurance companies.

- The legal obligations of pension fund fiduciaries have become increasingly clarified under ERISA and now MPERSA in the United States. Similar clarification processes are underway in the other major pension fund countries.

YES, BUT DOES IT WORK?

There is plenty of anecdotal evidence that the increased shareholder activism of U.S. pension funds in recent years has had a beneficial influence on corporate governance processes, both indirectly through funding corporate takeovers through LBO funds managed by such specialists as KKR, and through direct activism. Monks and Minow cite 25 direct activism cases involving pension funds in their book alone, involving such household corporate names as American Express, Borden Inc., Eastman Kodak, General Motors, Honeywell, IBM, Sears, RJR Nabisco, Texaco, and Westinghouse.

However, Monks and Minow also observe that most of this activism has come from relatively few public sector funds. Corporate funds continue to suffer from the fundamental contradiction that while in theory corporate fund fiduciaries are to act "solely in the best interests of the participants," this may be difficult in practice if they are also corporate employees.

Until recently, there has been little in the way of more rigorous academic research to back up the view that institutional activism has been beneficial to enhancing shareholder value. The findings of a 1997 study by Professor Mark Huson point in this direction.[15] Huson studied a sample of 18 firms targeted between 1990 and 1992 by the California Public Employees Retirement System (CalPERS) as poorly performing corporations.

Huson looked at the response of these 18 corporations to formal CalPERS targeting over the three years subsequent to their being targeted. He found that there was a significant change in the types of real activities announced by the targeted firms. Generally, these activities involved an increased number of announcements involving CEO and board changes, layoffs, divestitures, and joint ventures. The average market response to these announcements was measured to be more posi-tive in the posttargeting period than it had been in the pretargeting pe-riod. Huson concludes, "CalPERS intervention has a positive effect on the targeted firms' value."[16]

PENSION FUND CAPITALISM GOES GLOBAL

While the evolution toward pension fund capitalism taking place in the United States may be the most documented and visible among the developed economies, it is happening elsewhere too. To understand this evolution requires some prior history on the evolution of prepen-sion fund capitalism. Writing in the Winter 1997 issue of the *Journal of Applied Corporate Finance,* Franks and Mayer observe that prepen-sion fund capitalism evolved very differently in the United States and the United Kingdom compared with Germany, France, and Japan. They call the former "outsider" systems, and the latter "in-sider" systems.

Outsider systems are characterized by a large number of widely held public corporations and well-developed financial markets. Insider sys-tems, on the other hand, have fewer public corporations and less well-developed financial markets, with large share blocks in the hands of founding families, the banks, other corporations, or the government.[17] Writing in the same issue of the journal, Kaplan attempts to test the rel-ative effectiveness of outsider and insider systems. He finds that both systems are about equally effective at disciplining poor managerial per-formance but that outsider systems are more effective in discouraging successful companies from overinvesting.[18]

In yet another article in the Winter 1997 issue, Macey and Miller make what may be the most interesting observation of all: The outsider and insider systems are now beginning to converge, with the funding of pension systems a major convergence catalyst. They observe, for exam-ple, that German and Japanese corporations are beginning to make more use of public financial markets and to improve their standards of financial disclosure.

Through this process, domestic and foreign pension funds are increasing their investment exposure to these previously insider corporations. Meanwhile, domestic and foreign pension funds are for the first time creating an element of visible, concentrated ownership in many traditionally outsider corporations in the United States and the United Kingdom.[19] We would add that when in a developing economy, pension system funding is the primary driver creating public financial markets and an ownership class in that economy, the distinction between prior insider and outsider systems is moot. It was, for example, the pension system funding process itself that effectively created Chile's version of capitalism.

CONVERGENCE REVISITED

We observed in Chapter 1 that the world is converging on various forms of democratic capitalism as the guiding philosophy in how political and economic institutions are organized. We also noted that this convergence was occurring about 15 years ahead of the advent of the retirement of the outsized baby boomer generations in the developed economies. These two developments placed the spotlight directly on the role pension funds must play over the next 15 years and beyond. They must be reliable engines of wealth creation in a world that is increasingly shaped by free market forces, by inclusiveness, and by high levels of transparency and accountability in its public and private institutions.[20]

In this final chapter, we documented the increasing influence pension funds now exert on the way the world works. If the joint forces of democratic capitalism and boomer demographics turn out to be as irreversible as they appear, the economic power of pension funds can only continue to grow. However, an important message of this book is that potential economic power alone is not enough. Such potential power does not automatically equate to the growth in economic wealth pension fund stakeholders are counting on. To achieve that, fiduciaries must see the pension funds under their care as financial business with missions to create value for their stakeholders. Only the successful achievement of these missions many times over will produce the ultimate economic wealth we will all need in the twenty-first century.[21]

NOTES

1. *Pension Funds and Economic Power* by Paul Harbrecht SJ, (New York: The Twentieth Century Fund, 1959).

2. Ibid., page 270.

3. Ibid., page 271.

4. Drucker, See Chapter 1, note 6.

5. Harbrecht, op. cit., pages 233–234.

6. In her article "Public Pension Fund Activism in Corporate Governance Reconsidered" (*Columbia Law Review,* Vol. 93, No. 4, May 1993), Prof. Roberta Romano cites a number of such instances. They include a 1992 promise by (at that time) presidential candidate Bill Clinton to study how public fund assets might be used to finance infrastructure projects, a 1992 threat by the Illinois state treasurer to persuade public funds not to invest in LBO funds that caused job losses, and a 1989 New York state task force report titled "Our Money's Worth," which recommended restricting public fund involvement in hostile takeovers and instructing these funds to take local factors into account in their investment decisions.

7. In her study "The Use of Public Employee Retirement System Resources for Economic Development in the Great Lakes States" (Institute of Development Strategies, Indiana University, 1992), Prof. Jeanne Patterson found a portfolio of Economically Targeted Investments (ETIs) earned a return that was four percentage points below stock market returns over a five-year period. She concluded that the use of public retirement funds to subsidize economic development was inappropriate.

8. The most recent public study of the issue is *Canada's 20 percent Foreign Property Limit: Why and How It Should Be Removed* by Keith Ambachtsheer, September 1995. The study was funded jointly by the Pension Investment Association of Canada and the Investment Funds Institute of Canada. Canadian Finance Minister Paul Martin has indicated that the issue would be taken up in the formulation of the next phase of pension reform measures expected in 1998.

9. Usuki, See Chapter 16, note 5.

10. The sixth draft of the Management of Public Employee Retirement Systems Act went to the National Conference of Commissioners on Uniform

State Laws held in Sacramento, California, in August 1997, where it was passed by a strong vote. The challenge now is to get it adopted by the 50 state legislatures.

11. *Watching the Watchers* by Robert A. G. Monks and Nell Minow, (Cambridge, MA: Blackwell Publishers, 1996). The citation is from page 281.

12. The source of this information is the *Institutional Investment Report,* (Vol. 1, No. 1, January 1997) published by The Conference Board. Table 17.2 is a reproduction of Table 11 of the Report, page 38.

13. *The Modern Corporation and Private Property* by Adolf Berle and Gardiner Means, (New Brunswick, NJ: Transaction Publishers, 1991 ed.).

14. Monks and Minow, op. cit., pages 120–121.

15. *Does Governance Matter? Evidence from CalPERS Interventions* by Prof. Mark Huson, University of Alberta and University of Texas (Unpublished paper, April 1997). Citation is from the paper abstract on the cover sheet.

16. Robert Monks has done some creative work on the question of what the ideal "New Owner" of publicly traded corporations looks like. Eventually, he suggests, there might be institutions called "special purpose trust companies" (SPTCs) that specialize in discharging the growing ownership responsibilities of pension funds and other institutional investors. Their focus would be shareholder competency and independence from the various conflicts (potential or actual) that afflict public and corporate pension funds, and mutual funds.

17. The entire Winter 1997 issue of the *Journal of Applied Corporate Finance* (Vol. 9, No. 4) was devoted to international corporate governance issues. The title of the article by Julian Franks and Colin Mayer is "Corporate Ownership and Control in the United Kingdom, Germany and France."

18. From the same source as note 17, "Corporate Governance and Corporate Performance: A Comparison of Japan, Germany, and the United States" by Steven Kaplan.

19. From the same source as note 17, "Universal Banks Are Not the Answer to America's Corporate Governance 'Problem': A Look at Germany, Japan, and the U.S." by Jonathan Macey and Geoffrey Miller. Numerically, about half of the outstanding corporate shares in Japan are cross-held by other corporations. Of the remaining half, institutions hold about 50 percent. With deregulation of the Japanese pension system, that proportion is likely to rise. Canada provides an example of an interesting in-between case. Of the top 300 stocks listed on the Toronto Stock Exchange, about 20 percent of the shares are cross-held. Of the remaining 80 percent, institutions hold about half, with Canada's pension funds representing the most concentrated component. Again, with pension-related savings flows projected to

increase over the next decade, that level of concentration is likely to increase.

20. The most succinct, incisive analysis we have seen for the organizational implications of the convergence of the political, economic, technological, and demographic forces referred to in this book is contained in two essays titled "The New World" (November 1994) and "Culture: The Driving Force of the Twenty-first Century" (April 1997) by William A. Macdonald, President of W. A. Macdonald Associates Inc., a strategy and policy advisory firm based in Toronto, Canada.

21. Jane Ambachtsheer conducted much of the background research for this chapter.

Index